GET PAID TO WRITE!

3 PROVEN WAYS TO START MAKING MONEY NOW!!!

By T.J. ROHLEDER
America's Blue Jeans Millionaire

Table of Contents:

Introduction:

By T.J. Rohleder

T.J. Rohleder here! In this book, I'll introduce you to an exciting program called "Get Paid to Write," which outlines three little-known but very profitable writing methods that you can use to make enormous sums of money. **And how *much* money can you make? The sky's the limit!** You can easily make a six-figure income within a couple of years of getting started with our three methods—and I do mean easily. I say that with all the confidence in the world because we've used these methods to generate many millions of dollars in total revenues over the past few decades.

So when I say that you can make easily $100,000 or more within a couple of years with these methods, I mean it. And some people can make a lot more. **It all depends on how ambitious you are, what you're willing to do, and how well you put these strategies that I'm going to teach you into play.** Again, all three of these methods are virtually unknown. They're not taught in school; I don't think there are *any* colleges or universities that teach any of these methods.

And by the way, what these methods do *not* involve is something that a lot of you, I presume, are very interested in. When most people think about getting paid to write, they think of one thing and one thing only, and that's writing fiction. The truth is, I can't think of a harder way to make money than writing fiction. The market is overcrowded, there are so many talented people in the business, and you're at the mercy of all kinds of forces that are beyond your control. But if your dream *is* to write the Great American Novel and become rich and famous, **then my best advice to you is to go ahead and use these three methods that I'm going to teach you in this book anyway, as a way of making money while you're working on your novel on the side.**

You're still getting paid to write. That's the name of the game.

I'm going to say something to you now that you're going to hear me repeat numerous times throughout this program. Personally, I'm a very committed writer and so is Chris Lakey, my Marketing Director, who also contributed to the audio program on which this book is based. So I know that part of the attraction of writing is that you want to tap into your creative powers. **You want to make money creatively, while indulging your artistic expression and, sure, that's one of the greatest joys of writing.** Well, the three methods I'm going to talk about in this book all involve tremendous amounts of creativity. **In fact, you're only limited here by your imagination.**

When I say that some of you can go beyond a six-figure income, I'm talking about those of you who are willing to do more than most, who are willing to devote and dedicate themselves to these three methods, to commit their entire selves to them—really invest everything they've got. **That requires hard work, yes, but also that requires creativity. Simply put, the more creative you are, the more money you're going to make with these methods.** And while they all involve writing, a few of the things I'll discuss here—especially in connection with our third method, information marketing—are going to go beyond just the written word.

If your passion is to make money with fiction, I don't want to throw a wet blanket on your dreams. I'm not going be the one to tell you that you shouldn't do it. The history books' are filled with people whose desire to write fiction was so strong that they were willing to pay a tremendous price and, in so doing, they had Lady Luck smile upon them. **Think of J.K. Rowling and Stephen King, both of whom had humble beginnings... and now look at them.**

It happened to them and it can happen to you. **But my best advice is still to look at these three methods, think about them very carefully, and put them into play as you work your way toward fulfilling your fiction-writing dreams.** I know these methods work because they're the three methods that we use to generate our profits. We've been doing this for 23 years now, having started in 1988, and when we tell you that you can make an enormous income, we're speaking from our own experience. **We started with just $300, which we turned into over $10 million in total revenue within our first five years.** Many people have made even more money the same way—so much that our income pales by comparison. So I'm not bragging about our success *per se*. **I'm bragging about the methods and I want you to know that we're speaking from experience.**

In this book, I'll teach you the best of the best of what we've learned over the years. This is the kind of thing where you can make money super-fast and, better yet, you can earn while you learn. There are plenty of people out there using all three of these methods in combination. **I'm going to tell you a lot of stories throughout this book, things that I encourage you to spend a lot of time thinking about, highlighting, underlining, writing notes to yourself—however you learn**

best. And I'd recommend that you reread this book multiple times because, if you don't, you're shortchanging yourself.

I promise you, if you invest the time and read this book half a dozen times, you're going to notice things on that sixth time through that you didn't the first five times. **Those little things that you notice can make a big difference in your overall income.**

CHAPTER ONE:

Writing for Fun and Profit

One of my favorite things in the world is getting paid to write; the same is true for Chris Lakey, our Marketing Director. **We also love to teach other people about the strategies and principles that have made us money, and through this project, we're able to do both.** More than likely, you paid to receive this program; and that means that we had to convince you to buy it, which probably means that you received some sales copy that we wrote. Well, **one of the strategies that we'll be sharing with you here is copywriting.** When we wrote the sales copy that you looked at before you decided to make a purchase, we were exercising our writing ability. I'm going to teach you how to do the same thing.

True Profit Potential

In the introduction, I mentioned that most people who think of getting paid to write think first about writing fiction, and I was certainly no different. **Many people dream of writing at some point in their adolescence;** maybe it's all those papers we have to write in school, when we think, "Man, I should be getting paid to do this!" Some of us think that because we actually hate to write. **But some of us enjoy writing, and want to take it further.** I know a couple with a high school kid—I think he's 14 or 15 now—who just wrote his first book. It's fiction, of course, about 60,000 to 65,000 words long. I don't remember how long it took him from start to finish, but he worked on it for a long time. He's real proud of it; it's like his baby.

But will he make any money from it? That's doubtful. Even if the book is published, his parents might buy a copy, but very few other people will. The fiction-writing business is a tough gig. No matter how proud he is of his shiny new book, it's going to be hard to make money on it, even if he uses some of our connections to get it published. (And by the way, as side note, if you're interested in getting published on Amazon and being able to sell through the bookstores, we can help you with that.) **The reality is that's extremely difficult to make money with fiction, and very few people succeed at it.**

But there are enough people who do—people like the Stephen Kings and the J.K. Rowlings—to prove that it's possible. So there's good reason to have hope if you're into that kind of writing. **But I'm here to tell you about a different way. I'm here to tell you about what, in my opinion, is an *easier* way to profit from writing.** Is it foolproof? No. Does everybody in the field get rich? Certainly not. Does everybody make even a little money? Sadly, no. There are people who become writers who never make a dime. This is the reality of business. People get into all kinds of businesses that fail; **so if you're looking for a guaranteed way to make money, writing might not be it.**

And yet, as you'll find throughout the course of this book, these methods offer the *potential* to make a huge amount of money. And yes, it does take some effort; obviously, money doesn't grow on trees. If you want to get paid to write, you have to work at it... **but as you'll see in the principles and**

strategies that I'll share, the key to making the kind of money that you're looking for really is here. I don't know what your goals are, what your dreams are, but I do know that writing can help you get there; and unless you're the next Stephen King, writing nonfiction, is going to help you get there a lot faster.

The three methods that I'll outline in this book have worked very well for us. **We've been using these methods on a daily basis for decades; they've become integral parts of our money-making strategies.** And so these strategies, and the stories I'll use to illustrate them, all come from the heart — and as happy as that may sound, it's the truth. They're coming from what we know.

What I have to tell you can give you the power to transform your life, to make you all the money that you want. **Now, my approach may not be perfect and polished, but I know it works.** I'm not college educated; neither is Chris Lakey. We were both educated in the real world... and sometimes, that's a hard thing for people to swallow. People think that you need to have a four-year degree to succeed in business. I promise you that you don't. **Many of the world's most successful people, including self-made millionaires and billionaires, are not college-educated.** Oh, some of them have *some* college. Bill Gates dropped out of college. Chris Lakey went to college for a year at a small, private school.

But many successful entrepreneurs don't have fancy degrees. They don't have abbreviations behind their names. They don't have Ph.D.s or MBAs. **What they *do* have is real-world experience that can help teach you the things that you want to learn, and that you *need* to learn, to make a lot of**

money. That's something Chris and I have.

I believe that what I offer here is an exciting ride, and that you're going to have a lot of fun as I teach you about making money and getting paid to write. **Even though some the strategies may be unconventional, and even if you came into this thinking that you wanted to be a fiction writer, we can guide you to profitability.** You can still write your fiction; but if you want to make the most money as a writer, you need to consider nonfiction, and you need to take a good, hard look at the three ways of doing so that I'm going to share with you in this book. **I guarantee you that you can make money off your writing, if you'll just follow our simple guidelines.**

The Reality of Copywriting

It's a truism that somebody can only teach you what they know. In medical school, they like to say: "See one, do one, teach one." That gives you some practical experience that really means something. Otherwise it's just theory coming out of a textbook, and you can get that in school all day long.

Here at M.O.R.E., Inc., we actually practice what we preach. I have to admit, though, that the kind of writing we do irritates English teachers—especially the first method I'll teach you, which is copywriting. Copywriters are famous for upsetting English teachers. **We don't worry about grammar because when you're writing sales copy, you're writing as you speak.** Something that sounds good often violates all kinds of grammar rules. But that's acceptable, because **part of the secret of writing good advertising copy is to create a bond with someone, to establish a warm, personal relationship with them.** If you're too stiff with your writing, if everything is perfect and homogenized and careful, then you're not going to make any impact. They're probably not even going to read it. If they do, they're not going to buy from you.

The kind of copywriting that we teach is called direct response copywriting, or direct response marketing copywriting. Its name indicates what it's all about: getting a direct response. **Your goal is to cause people to take action; you're looking for a profitable response.** There are plenty of direct response copywriters who are making tremendous amounts of money, and they do it in two different ways: **you can either use your skills to sell your own products and services, which is what we do, or you can become a freelance copywriter.** Let's get the latter out of the way first.

Chris has done a little freelance copywriting, but I've never wanted to do so, because I'm an entrepreneur—which is to say, I'm unemployable. **I'm so used to working for myself that there's no way I would ever be happy working for someone else.** And when you're a freelancer, you *are* working for someone else, and you've got to take crap from clients. Well, I became self-employed so I could be my own boss and never have to answer to anybody again. Admittedly, that's a kind of immature thinking... but I started my first business when I was basically a kid. Nowadays I'm much more mature in my thinking (not that I'm there all the way), so I realize that I'm accountable to all the people on my team, and to my suppliers and, of course, my customers; but I just never had a real interest in freelance work. Still, it's nice to know that I could do it if I ever needed to. And it can be quite profitable; **some freelancers charge thousands of dollars just to write simple sales letters and website copy.**

If you have a desire to do freelance work, there's a ton of it out there, and most business people can use your help. You see, they might know a lot about the market they're in and the products and services they sell, but when it comes to expressing themselves on paper or on a website, most of them can't write worth a damn. **They just don't have it within them to write. Now, they could, potentially; anybody can become a writer if they're serious about it.** Hey, if I can write, anybody can. But most people have never developed that skill or ability. Maybe they're afraid to put words on paper, because whenever they try it, they're no good at it.

Every business in the world needs more sales and profits. If they're already doing well, they want to do better; and if they're struggling, then they need to generate *more* sales and profits. That's the solution to every cashflow or business crisis. So there's a huge need here, and a huge demand: there are tens of millions of businesses in the U.S. alone. **We're going to tell you about all kinds of different ways that you can get freelance work, if that's what you want to do.** And remember this, always: even the guys who are charging thousands of dollars to write direct mail packages all started in the same place you're going to start. They didn't know anything about the field, at first. Now, years later, they're experts—and you can learn to be one too.

The kind of copywriting that I'm going to be talking the most about, however, is the method of writing your own sales copy to sell your own products and services. I wrote my very first direct response marketing display ad back in the summer of 1988, and I'll never forget it. I spent the whole weekend writing one tiny sixth-page piece, a two-inch by three-inch column ad.

Why did I spend all weekend doing it? Because I'm a perfectionist, and it was the only $300 I had at the time, and didn't want to blow it. I didn't want to place those ads only to have them not work.

So I laid out all these existing ads, and I studied everything about them. We knew our market very well, especially the magazines that we were going to advertise in. I'd bought a lot of stuff from a lot of companies that were selling similar types of things. **So I applied all those examples and all that knowledge, and put a lot of time and energy and thought into writing maybe 50 words.** That was it. Heck, there might not have been even 50 words... yet that little ad was the spark that started our mighty fire, because we took the profits from that ad and kept pyramiding them into more little ads, and then bigger ads, and then into direct mail—and **within five years we had brought in over $10 million.**

From that point forward, I learned how to write sales letters. My very first sales letter was the initial lead fulfillment for that ad, which I sent to them when they responded to the ad. But beyond that, I had an idea for a product called the $2,500 Weekend. I'll tell you more about it as we go into the copywriting segment. **The product only took a weekend to create, with the help of my wife and marketing expert Russ von Hoelscher... and then I spent three months working on the sales letter.**

Why did I spend three months? Because I was new to it, and I'm a perfectionist. **I wanted to do it right. I wanted it to be *perfect*, so I did the best I could.** I could do that same job now in as little as three or four days if I had to bang it out right away. I spent three months on it then, though, because I was new to the business; and yet, **that letter ultimately generated $1.5 million in sales.** That was the first product we ever created that made over one million dollars. Since then, we've had a bunch of them.

This was right before the Internet took off in the early 1990s. **Back then, there were these things called computer bulletin boards, precursors to the Internet.** Well, there were a bunch of people who were advertising on these computer bulletin boards for free. **When we found out about this, I hooked up with some people who were knowledgeable in the field, and we created a product.** Then I wrote a sales letter. Again, it took me three or four months to write it, so I was really taking the time to get it right. But compared to writing a novel, which people will sometimes spend three or four years writing, or even 10 years, three or four months is nothing.

This letter generated $2.5 million within six months... and then the Internet hit big-time, and the new World Wide Web basically put all the computer bulletin boards out of business. There were about 60,000 computer bulletin boards before then... but when the Web took off, the whole bulletin boards industry was just wiped out. Well, I wasn't. **I simply rewrote that bulletin boards sales letter to fit this new Internet phenomenon, and we generated over $12 million more that we split with our joint venture partner.** All that just from rewriting a letter!

The ability to recycle your sales material is something I'm going to talk about a lot in this book. I've got a letter right now that I wrote 14 years ago; it was originally called "Part Time Wealth." We mailed out millions of copies of this letter, and we made a lot of money with it back then. Recently, Chris Lakey took that same sales letter, rewrote it slightly, added his own brilliance to it, and made it into a 17-minute movie that he put on the Internet. Again, you can recycle all of this stuff! **If you're selling your own products and services to the same market, then a good sales letter can be used repeatedly.** You know, I think we've probably mailed 20 or 30 million copies of that letter; it was recycled again and again. That's one of the secrets of effective copywriting when you're selling your own products and services, assuming your market is big enough.

Right now, we're looking at a huge product that we're selling to businesses. **Our market there is potentially as many as 10 million businesses, so just one good sales letter could potentially be mailed to that market millions of times in various forms.** This is good news, because remember: you're getting paid on the sale of the product or service, not necessarily the time that you spent writing the sales letter; **so even if it only takes you a few hours to revise an existing letter, it can pay off with millions and millions of dollars.**

That's one of the reasons I want you to consider copywriting. Now, I'm very sensitive about the fact that you may have purchased this book with no real intention, necessarily, to start a business or sell products and services. **That's fine: you could still be a freelance copywriter.** You'll be self-employed, but at least you won't be at the mercy of publishing companies, depending on them to sell your work. **You'll be taking charge of your own life.** I just can't think of a worse way to make money than by spending several years writing a good book on speculation, putting your whole heart and soul into it, and then expecting a publisher to sell it on your behalf when they've got a whole stable of other writers out there.

I hate that idea. Think about what a weak position that puts you in, compared to the strong position of learning how to take that talent you have for writing and using it to sell products and services. You can do this either for yourself or for other businesses that need help, businesses that would value and appreciate you and pay you very well for writing direct response copy. As I mentioned briefly, Chris Lakey has had the experience of doing both freelance and personal copywriting. **Each has its benefits and drawbacks, and you have to weigh them in the balance and decide what works best for you.** Consider the arguments I make for both methods throughout this book, and decide for yourself which would be most interesting to you. You may decide to do some of both.

When writing sales copy for other people, you have a certain obligation to be very good at your job; whereas, if you were writing for yourself, you don't have anybody else to be accountable to. If you write for your own business, or for your own products or services, and things don't work out... well, you just dust yourself off, go back to the drawing board, and try again. If you're writing for somebody else, then you're accountable to them. You have to decide: do you offer a guarantee of some kind, or not? Do they have to sign something saying they understand that there are all kinds of variables that are beyond your control, and that your copy is not guaranteed? **Of course, you never can really guarantee *anything* in business.** Even if you write a killer sales letter, there's no guarantee, for example, that they're going to mail it to the right list. **So you do have to deal with certain expectations.**

If you write sales copy for another company or another individual, of course they'll want you to do a good job. They'll hold you accountable if you don't. Maybe all that means is that you don't get their business again; but maybe it means they want you to give them some or all of their money back. **There are all kinds of variables to consider when you're writing for someone else.**

Another consideration when you're writing for somebody else is that you have to do the research necessary to get to know their marketplace. When you're writing to your own customers, you tend to have all the answers for whatever people are concerned about in that marketplace. **If you're writing for somebody else, you have to do enough research to get inside their customers' heads.** It's a different animal, a different ball game, and maybe you take more time to write the copy because of the extra research required. For example, if you were to become a copywriter for products that you had no personal experience with, no firsthand knowledge of, you would first probably have to get your hands on the products in order to get to know them a little better. **You'd also have to do research to get a thorough understanding of the buyers in that marketplace—all before you even wrote your first word.**

So there's a considerable amount of time and effort involved in just getting to know the marketplace you're trying to sell to, assuming you don't already have experience with it. **The good news is that the best freelance copywriters demand a pretty hefty fee.** In fact, you could get paid thousands of dollars—even tens of thousands of dollars—to write one sales letter or one ad. **Some of the best copywriters even demand royalty payments.** That is, if you're writing for somebody else and that ad generates a million dollars, maybe you get one percent of that as a bonus, or five percent as a royalty. You're worth the bonus in that case. If your ad becomes a winner and runs all over the U.S., generating millions of dollars in revenue, then you've understood the marketplace very well. You wrote a killer ad, and orders are coming in like gangbusters.

Now, that doesn't happen often; most people just charge a flat fee for copywriting. But some people do negotiate royalty payments as well. When you write for other people, you do have that profit potential; just one sales letter can make you a lot of money, once you've worked your way up to the point of true expertise. I'm not saying that you'll land those kinds of writing gigs when you first get started... but you never know. **All you can do is keep writing and doing what you love, looking for opportunities to sell your services to other people.**

But in my opinion, it really is far better to write for yourself, pushing your own products and services. **One of the coolest things about writing for yourself is that all the royalties earned by your copy are yours alone. You can write a sales letter once and mail it for weeks, or months, or years, depending on the offer and what you're selling, and money can continue to come in all that time.** Let's say you're selling a widget, and that you wrote your own sales letter for it. It's your widget; you either have the rights to sell it, or you invented it. Let's say that on every $50 widget sale, you get to keep half of that after your expenses to manufacture and ship the widget. That's $25 profit on every widget order. So your sales copy is working like crazy, and orders are pouring in. If you make a million dollars on this widget over several months' time, and you get to keep half of that, then you've made half a million bucks.

So it's your choice: should you write copy for someone else, or just for yourself? **Either way can be profitable, and** you can do both simultaneously—focusing on your own hot products, for example, while selling your services as a freelance copywriter on the side. Either way, it's exciting to put words on paper or a website that cause people to send you cash, checks, and money orders, and to pull out their credit cards for you to charge. **It's perpetually thrilling... and it really is only limited by your imagination.**

The Ghostly Option

Our second way to get paid to write is the one that I'm going to go into the least detail about; in fact, I'll discuss it only in one chapter. But it's still a valuable way to make money, and some writers build their entire careers around it. Again, it's something that you can do for other people, but there are other ways that you can make money with it, which we'll also explain.

This second method is ghostwriting. Ghostwriting is simply you writing for other people under *their* names, something like the way a speechwriter writes speeches for a politician. A ghostwriter writes all kinds of things, though; and people need ghostwriters, desperately, because most just can't write. To be honest, they suck at it. The world is just filled with bad writers... which is terrible for them. **They *need* your writing skills to promote themselves, to promote their ideas—to become famous in their marketplaces, whatever those may be.** Politicians need voters. Businesses need customers and clients. **And then there are plenty of companies like ours, who need ghostwriters to write stuff so that we can sell it.** Here at M.O.R.E., Inc., we've been using ghostwriters almost from the very beginning of our business. Within the first four or five months, we were having ghostwriters produce little manuals for us that were then sold by our distributors. Later, we used ghostwriters to produce all kinds of booklets, books, and reports.

Our first ghostwriter, Steve Lockman, wrote dozens of manuals, books, and reports for us, and helped us earn millions of dollars worth of sales—and he worked for a very reasonable price, and never asked for a royalty. We'd tell him what kind of manual we wanted, and he did all of his own research. Then, about five or six years ago, we were lucky enough to meet our current ghostwriter: a man named Floyd Largent out of San Antonio, Texas. **Floyd is a brilliant writer. He takes all the audio transcripts we produce**—including the transcripts for the audio program we're recording right now for *Get Paid to Write*—**and turns them into books, reports, and the like.** In this case, we'll probably also use some of the copy he returns for newsletters and other types of products.

We found Floyd through a web site called Elance.com. We just posted an ad telling people that we needed a ghostwriter to produce thousands of pages for us over a long term period. A total of 34 different writers applied, and we narrowed that field down to the three that we thought were the best. We gave each a little job, and two of them were absolutely terrible. Floyd stood out as the diamond we were looking for, and we've been working with him ever since. **He's ghostwritten literally thousands of pages that we've used for newsletters, reports, books, and all kinds of products—including this one.**

So that's how we've used ghostwriters over the years. It's a great profession, and it's something that's badly needed. **If it's something that interests you, then we can help you make more money with ghostwriting.** We can help you reach business people, so you can help them write certain books that

WRITING FOR FUN AND PROFIT 23

will draw the right clientele to them. We can show you how to write for politicians who need to attract voters. Just think about it: so many people would love to have a book of their own. They've always thought about it, they've fantasized about it, and yet they simply don't have the writing skills to produce one. **But you can. And it can be as easy as just interviewing these people, having the transcripts typed up, and then simply rewriting those transcripts with a little help from the client.**

Ghostwriters can make tremendous amounts of money. **You can either tap into this option as a way to increase your profits as you do your other writing, or make it a full-time writing business.** As I've said, there's a huge demand for them. Now, you may not realize that this is the case, because in a sense, ghostwriters are stealth writers. They fly under your radar... but you've encountered their work. You've probably encountered a lot of it.

Think about it; I'm guessing that you've encountered one of these scenarios. You're a sports fan, let's say, and you have a favorite athlete. You love to watch them play their sport, and you enjoy hearing them be interviewed... and you learn that they also have a book. But you know, because you've heard them talk, that there's no way they could write a book; they can hardly complete full sentences. You know that they must have skated through school on scholarships. They never really learned much, because they didn't have to; they've always been a talented athlete. And yet, they wrote a book. Yeah, right! **You know in your heart that somebody else wrote that book for them. They didn't do it; there's no way.** You've heard them talk before; you've heard them interviewed. They're good on the field, or on the court, or in the pool, or whatever sport it is... but there's no way they wrote their own book. **They've got a ghostwriter.**

Here's another scenario. Maybe you're not a sports fan, but you follow politics. Maybe you follow a particular person; you've heard them speak, both in recordings and live. You know that there's no way they could have written a book. They're not smart enough to write like that. They can barely get a whole thought out and write a paragraph, let alone pen a book. You know this because you've heard them talk, or you've seen them on the stage, or you've heard them on TV, or the radio, or whatever the case may be. **You know that these people have** *other* **people writing their books for them.**

So you've encountered this kind of writing before, knowingly or not. Maybe you just didn't think about it like that, or you never realized how big it is. But it's huge, really. **People from all walks of life have other people write their books for them. Celebrities do it all the time.** You've seen these people on Letterman and Leno; maybe they can act, but in real life they're kind of ditzy. Whenever someone asks them a question, they sound like a complete boob. If they've got a book out, then most likely they have someone else writing for them.

That's where ghostwriting comes in. It's widely used, but mostly the people doing it are unknown. The work behind the scenes. If you're the kind of person who wants fame and glory, then you should probably avoid this writing method. **But if you just want the cash, and you don't care about getting the fame or the glory, the world's your oyster.** There are huge numbers of people—athletes, politicians, Hollywood actors, famous people, as well as average Joes, people just like you and me—who just want to have a book of their own, but don't have a way to write it themselves. **There's a huge gap out there of people that want books, but can't write them.** You can come in and fill that gap as a ghostwriter, offering them something that they can't otherwise get.

Some of the best ghostwriters make huge amounts of money, especially those who ghost for celebrities or politicians. If you can get into those circles, you can have people who pay you to write their big political novel; and even if it isn't a novel, it probably contains a little fiction, even if they mean it to be nonfiction. Whether you're talking political types or Hollywood types, they're making so much money that they don't know what to do with it anyway—and so they might as well give it to you to be a ghostwriter for them. Pen their memoir, or just write about their favorite Chihuahua, or whatever it is; who knows? **They want someone to write a book because they were told they should *have* a book. They know they can go out on the circuit, go on the talk shows, sell some copies of their book, and make more money.** They're happy to give some of that to a ghostwriter to do all the work for them.

So, if you're interested in writing at all as a ghostwriter and don't mind the fact that, in most cases, no one will know who you are, this is a very lucrative business to get into. Later in the book, we'll share some stories about some people who are ghostwriters, and talk about how much money they've made. Check it out. Imagine being called on to write a book about some famous Hollywood type or some athlete. You get to know them, you get to interview them, you talk on the phone to them, you're in the editing stages with them. Maybe you meet them and end up doing some face-to-face work. Or maybe you're working through their agent; but you still get to rub shoulders with famous people.

You're behind the scenes. Accept that. Their name is on the cover, but you know the words are all yours, even if you wrote in a style that reflects their personal style. That could be exciting; it could be fun and new and different all the time, and pay extremely well. It could provide a lifetime of profits for you.

Information Marketing

The final method of getting get paid to write is the one that we'll spent the most time with, and you'll see that towards the end of the book. This is the method known as information marketing.

When we first started our business back in 1988, we called ourselves self publishers. Nowadays, we think of ourselves more holistically; we pursue many other media, including the Internet and audio. You see, information marketing encompasses all different kinds of products, and part of what we're going to teach you is to get beyond your initial preconceptions of exactly what it is. **Ultimately, in fact, we're going to tell you about over 40 different types of information products that you can create and market.**

Information marketing can be extremely lucrative, especially when combined with ghostwriting and copywriting. I know that for a fact, because this combination has been the basis of our success here at M.O.R.E., Inc. That's how we grew from a grubstake of just $300 in the beginning—which was all the money that my wife and I had at the time—to a gross income of over $140 million in less than 23 years. Again, I don't say that to brag; I'm bragging on the methods, though.

Information marketing can just be incredibly profitable, in large part because unique information products, items that you and you alone create, give you a way to differentiate yourself in the market. Your product has no real competition, if only because you're a part of that product. **Add in the fact that the marketplace is absolutely insatiable, and you have a winning recipe.** Many people who buy information products become habitual re-buyers. They get hooked on it.

I'm one of these people. I spend thousands of dollars every year buying all kinds of information products, because I'm addicted to learning. For instance, I can't drive in my car without listening to audio, so I'm always buying seminars and programs that other people produce. I'm always trying to get an edge. **I'm trying to learn constantly—and so I'm a typical information buyer.** I'm insatiable. The more I buy, the more it increases my hunger to buy more. I continue to spend money. I've spent God only knows how many hundreds of thousands of dollars on information products, and thank goodness I represent a huge and growing market of other repeat buyers—people who keep buying once they get hooked on these information products. **The more they buy, the more they *want* to buy.**

And by the way, that's a pretty good addiction. It only has a few negative side effects; for example, after a while you end up with an enormous library. There's no way you can go through it all, and you do tend to spend a lot of money. **But when you're on the other side of the cash register, and you're now selling to people who are addicted to buying information products like you are, then it's a great business to be in. People are looking for results.** You bought this program because you're looking for a way to get paid to write. Ambitious people who buy these information products as part of our ambition... well, we just can't get enough. We have to get more constantly.

The Internet has made this industry explode with growth, so it's more lucrative than ever. There are more people selling information now than ever before in history—but don't let that be a turn-off to you. **It should be a turn-on instead, because it means that the market is vibrant and active enough to be able to support all those people. If you can just learn to outcompete some of them, you've got it made!** Now, admittedly, the fact that there *are* a lot of people out there making money in the market does tend to make things a little challenging in the beginning. **But if you distinguish yourself and learn to exploit niches, you can make a fortune.**

Right now, after 23 years in business, we're entering a brand-new market sector ourselves, selling primarily to businesses. We've been in the consumer market since '88, but now our emphasis is shifting. We do have a varied mix of customers, of course, and some of our customers are businesspeople already; so I'm not saying that we've never sold to businesses. **But now we're aiming directly at businesses, and yes, there's already a ton of information sellers out there selling to businesses—but we think that's a damn good thing.** We're excited about that. Those people have warmed our customers up. Those people have taken care of all the preliminaries necessary for us to come in and sell our prospects additional, related products that give them the results they want. **In this case, all the products and services we're developing are intended to teach them how to make more money in their businesses, which is something every business owner or manager wants.**

I think that you should give some serious consideration to information marketing, if only because you can do so much with it in so many different ways. That's part of the challenge in it: that it can be anything you want it to be. These days, it's so easy to produce information, right at your desk. For example, Chris Lakey has a fairly inexpensive Mac computer that he creates products on. He's got a studio-quality microphone plugged into that Mac that's probably more expensive than it needs to be, but nevertheless wasn't all that expensive. A little USB bridge connects it straight into his computer. He has a camera that he can use to record high-definition video, or standard definition video if he chooses.

With that set-up, Chris can produce just about any kind of information product he might want to. Now, maybe he needs a graphic artist to help him make it all nice and slick, or he might need help laying out a book. But the basic production part he can handle himself, just by writing copy on a word processing program or by recording a quick audio or video program. **Basically, video, audio, and print covers all kinds of variables on any subject that Chris, or I, might want to create products for.**

Writing is the hardest part, in my opinion. But if you want, you can just sit down and record an audio file into your computer. You might have someone else, like a ghostwriter (as we talked about earlier) turn your audio into print; or you could just sell the audio product. Or you could point that webcam at yourself and record a video clip. **In short, you could create an information product with ease.** It's so easy now compared to how it used to be, which means that everybody can do it.

For whatever reason, most people, even those with the inclination to do so, still don't try. Part of the reason may be that they think it's too easy—that if it's so easy, it can't be worth anything, and therefore this isn't the best field to get into. They're selecting themselves out of the market... which makes it easier for those of us willing to take the chance. Even though there are many people serving just about every decent marketplace via information marketing, **because it *is* easier than ever before, the field is still wide open.** There's plenty of room for new people, especially in the niche businesses where you can reach these small groups of customers with specialized messages and products.

Once you create a marketplace for yourself, once you've carved out that niche that you start serving customers, you'll find that they're insatiable. **If they buy one thing, they'll probably buy all kinds of products related to what they've already purchased.** So if you sold them a book, they might be interested in an audio program on a similar subject, or a DVD, or something like that. Maybe they'll subscribe to a newsletter.

In the section in which I discuss information publishing, toward the end of the book, I'll give you over 40 examples of information products that you can produce—and a lot of them are very easy. **The ideas they're based on are easy, too. It's just a matter of you deciding that you want to implement them, and then getting with it. You'll definitely want to give deep consideration to information marketing, folks; and I'll provide plenty of information on the topic, never fear.** In fact, when you get right down to it, this very *Get Paid to Write* program is an example of information marketing and information publishing—so you've got an example all wrapped up in this book you're reading now.

It's just another example of what you should consider as you think about getting paid to write. **As we've said, we incorporate all three of these things into our business almost on a daily basis.** We're writing copy. We have ghostwriters working for us. All that's integral to our information marketing efforts. They're all things we do on a regular basis.

Dive Right In

If you read any of these segments and they really get you excited, and you want more information, then we probably already have other products available that we could point you to—or we may have coaching opportunities and other possibilities that we can make available to you, to help you delve into an advanced study of any of these methods. Again, I want to congratulate you for buying this book, and realize: this is only the beginning. **In order to get the most out of it, let this be only one of many times that you reread and closely consider this material. Pick and choose what works best for you.** If ghostwriting excites you, reread that chapter again and again; if information marketing appeals to you more, focus on those chapters. Write in the margins. Highlight passages. Use bookmarks and sticky notes. Don't just read this once and forget it.

Find what excites you, and then get started. Don't expect to be great from the get-go: as the saying goes, "It doesn't have to be good, it just has to be good enough." **In our business, you don't strive for perfection, because it's not profitable to do so. Just get moving, and strive to get something out there. Keep moving forward, and you'll get better as you go.**

I laugh at some of the early sales copy I wrote, because compared to what I can do today, the quality of that early work just embarrasses me. It was good enough at the time, and it was something, and most of it made us money; but I like what I do today better. **Your business is a journey that you're on, and each of the products you produce represents one of many different steps along the way.**

So don't worry about it being perfect at this point. Don't worry about your products being as good as they might be. **Do your best, of course, but just get something done and start moving.** Don't be frozen by the paralysis of analysis, or the bugaboo of perfectionism. **Start selling your work right away,** whether you're copywriting, ghostwriting, self-publishing information products, or all of the above. Whatever you're doing, just keep moving forward, and it'll come. **We're here to help as much as you want and as often as you like.** Just let us know how we can serve you and we'll be happy to accommodate!

You see, our goal for this entire program, including this book, is kind of lofty. **We really want to change some lives here.** Sure, we're selling this program to make a profit; you know it and I know it. That's why we're in business. **And yet, what we have to share with you is about more than just making money.** It's about you living your ideal lifestyle as a writer, getting paid to write, doing what you love, putting words on paper or a website or, if you're listening to this decades from now, God only knows where you'll be putting those words! **Whatever the medium, it's still about taking the talent, the skill, the ability, that unique part of who you are, and expressing it in such a way that you're paid for it.** That is *so* much better than depending on an outside publisher to do it for you, though again, if you have those desires, you have a way now to supplement your income while you're waiting for that big break that you're looking for.

By investing in this book, you're really investing in yourself. That's why I encourage you to go through it more than once, focusing on those things you're most interested in. **And don't forget, we're here for you.** We're here to serve you. So take advantage of that

Chapter Two:

Why You Should Become a Copywriter

In the next few chapters, I'm going to talk about how you can get into the profitable field of copywriting. Specifically, what we teach here at M.O.R.E., Inc. is the direct response variety of copywriting. You see, there's quite a difference between the plain kind of copy that you see a lot of businesses using—not just local businesses, but even national businesses—and the kind of copy that *we* write.

Direct response copy is simply a compelling sales message coupled with a specific call to action. In fact, the purpose of *all* the copywriting we do is to get people to take some type of action—to pick up a phone and call, to send for a free DVD or an audio CD, or to purchase a small product that indicates their interest in what we're offering. That's the only kind of copywriting that we understand and have ever used, and we've made well over one hundred million dollars by using it.

I have a lot of great stories to tell, and I'm hoping those stories will inspire you.

Let's start by talking about why you should want to learn to write good direct response copy. **After all, the "why" to do something is always more important than the "how" to do it.** This field is full of great "whys," and I think it's definitely something for you to get excited about. **So I've got four main**

reasons for why you should think about becoming a
copywriter: it's fun, it's lucrative, it's challenging, and it's
creative.

The Joy of Copywriting

Let's look at the fun part first. You write an ad, you place
it in a magazine or a newspaper, and then you sit back and you
wait for the money. Or you write a sales letter and mail it out to a
group of prospective buyers, and then you just wait and see what's
going to happen. **Our good friend, Eric Bechtold, compares
copywriting to a combination of fishing and chess.** I've always
loved that metaphor, because **fishing is fun;** lots of people do it in
their spare time as a hobby. It's certainly not something that
people really work at, it's just something that they enjoy.

Then, of course, there's chess—a game filled with many
different complexities. **It can be quite complicated.** I don't want
to dampen your spirits here, but as with all types of writing,
there's a lot to learn when it comes to copywriting. **It's like chess
in that you can spend your entire life devoted to becoming the
best you can possibly be, and** *still* **not know it all.** I don't say
that to discourage you. In fact, one of the things I'm going to talk
about a little bit later is the challenge of it all. I find it very
satisfying to know that you can never know everything about
copywriting, that you're always going to be learning something
new. That's part of what makes it so much fun.

**The very first advertisement I wrote, 23 years ago, took
me a whole weekend to put together.** I call that "the weekend
that changed my life." It was just one-sixth of a page in size, and
we placed it in two national magazines owned by the same
company. One-sixth of a page is very small, approximately two

by three inches... and yet I spent a whole weekend writing that tiny ad, something I could do now in five minutes!

What did I do for a whole weekend? First, I clipped out a whole bunch of other ads that I'd seen over the years in those same publications, and I spread them out all over the floor. **Then I selected little bits and pieces that I liked about those ads—the way that this one was presented, the way that one was designed, and some of the copy from here and from there.** Ultimately, I worried a lot. We had a very small amount of money to work with at the time; my wife and I were struggling financially. These two ads represented just about all the money we had, in fact, and we couldn't afford to just waste it. So I spent a whole weekend fretting... but also having fun. Writing copy is very creative work—an aspect that I'm also going to touch on later—and you can get absorbed in it. Hours turn into minutes, days turn into hours.

Ultimately, that little ad earned us $10 million within less than five years. It was that spark that started the mighty fire for us. I wrote that ad, and then I wrote a sales letter to the people that responded to it. That's as simple as it still can be. That was almost a quarter of a century ago, and yet it's still just that simple: **you write an ad, people send for materials, and you write a sales letter. Basically, that's it.** At the time, we were selling a little booklet that sold for $12.95. That was our humble beginning... and yet we made a nice profit on those two ads. We used those profits to buy four ads, and the profits from those four ads to buy eight. Pretty soon, we wrote a full-page ad. By the time we were in business for six months, we were bringing in an average of $500 a day. By then we'd hired a consultant, Russ von Hoelscher of El Cajon, California, to work with us.

I remember sweating over that full-page ad as I wrote it. It probably took me about a week, because again, I fretted over every little thing and rewrote it over and over. Then I showed it to Russ and asked if he would tweak it—if he would make suggestions and a few changes. And he did. He wrote a whole new headline for it that was a million times better than mine. And I'll never forget that Russ said to me, "Why didn't you just let me write the ad?" That comment has always stuck in my mind.

Well, the reason I didn't let him write the ad is because I wanted to learn how to do it myself. I've always had a fascination with those sales letters and ads that I'd read over the years, the ones that got me so excited that I sent in my money. **I just thought, "What a cool, fun way to make money!** You can write an ad or a sales letter, people see it, and they respond by giving you money—just because of the words that you wrote!" I thought that was cool 23 years ago, and I still think it's cool today. **Sure, it's a challenge to write sales copy, but the fun comes in when you anticipate the results of that copy you've written.** I suppose if you write a book, there's some anticipation between the time the book is finished and the time it actually gets published. But I don't imagine it's anywhere *near* as exciting as the time between writing your copy and its appearance in the mail or a newspaper or a magazine. And then, of course, there's the joy of having the money flow in! **The ability to turn words into cash, to know that every ad or sales letter you run is going to produce a certain result... that's thrilling.**

Copywriting is Lucrative

Copywriting can make you a boatload of money, which is the second reason why you should do it. Now, when you hear people discussing the idea of getting paid to write, most just don't think about writing sales copy. Usually, they think of fiction—even though fiction-writing doesn't make people much money at all. A very limited number of the people who write novels make decent amounts of money; they're the famous authors that everyone knows about. A few people may think of non-fiction, if they're interested in that sort of thing, but in general, writing non-fiction isn't much better. Most book-length works just don't sell that well; that's why there are whole stores full of leftover, remaindered books.

Copywriting is a much more lucrative proposition. This is true whether you're writing sales copy to sell your own products and services, or writing for hire. Some freelance copywriters are earning tremendous amounts of money—thousands of dollars for a direct mail package. People who are unfamiliar with direct response marketing often call what we do "junk mail." That's the stuff that comes in the mail that normally hits the trashcan immediately. **Well, we call it "direct mail"—and there are plenty of copywriters who are getting paid thousands of dollars to write one good direct mail package.** A lot of copywriters who write for other people get paid a flat fee, but in some cases, they get paid a royalty based on the gross number of sales that come in from the ad or sales letter that they write— which, again, can be a very lucrative way to make money.

Now, that's a little more difficult than writing for yourself, because when you're writing to sell your own product or service, you tend to be more passionate about it; and you're definitely more knowledgeable about it. If you want to write a sales letter to sell someone else's product, you first have to learn about their product and the marketplace they're selling to. **It's**

much more difficult to write sales copy for a product you don't have any firsthand knowledge of than it is to write for something that's your own baby.

I understood this almost from the very beginning. After we started working with Russ von Hoelscher, I could have let him write my sales letters. At that point, Russ had been a freelance copywriter for about 20 years, so he would have done a fine job of it. But as I mentioned earlier, I was determined to learn how to do it myself. **So we ran that full page ad, and then Russ helped us get involved in direct mail—which opened up whole new avenues of profitability.** Direct mail let us reach so many more people in a much more powerful way.

You see, there are mailing lists out there with the names of millions of prospective buyers on them. **All you have to do is write a sales letter and send it out to a relatively small number of those people, so you can get a good test.** If it's something that the larger group of people wants to buy, they will pay you money directly, or you can use what we call two-step marketing to get them to take a small initial step, and then follow up with more sales copy that asks them for the larger amount of money that you want.

Within five years of Russ turning us on to direct mail, we had generated over $10,000,000. There really is a fortune to be made writing sales copy, and our company is proof of it! **Good copywriting causes people to take action by getting them excited about whatever it is that you're offering. Your *words* do that to people.** They make an emotional impact. People read your ads, they read your sales letters, and they get excited because of what you wrote. They send you the money, or they take the action that you want them take. It's the most awesome feeling in the world... and it's also profitable.

I don't consider myself to be a good writer at all. I struggle with my writing. For that reason, **I'm of the belief that if I can do it, then anybody can**—and not to brag, but many of my sales letters have generated over $1,000,000 each. That's power. **To get an idea and then write a sales letter and have it generate tens of thousands or hundreds of thousands of dollars, or even over $1,000,000, is the most powerful feeling I personally know.** This is especially true if you're writing copy for yourself. You might not necessarily feel the power if you're doing this as a freelancer... but if you're writing copy to sell your own products and services, then you *do* have the ability to make millions of dollars with the words that you write. Nobody can sell it like you can. **If you're selling something that's yours, something that you believe in, it's just a matter of transferring your belief in that product or service to other people. Your words make all that happen.**

Russ used to come to our home and spend the weekend helping us put together copy. This was when we were still struggling; we were bringing in thousands of dollars a month, but we certainly hadn't generated millions of dollars at this point. We had been in the business for less than a year. We'd pick him up at the airport on a Friday night, he would spend the weekend at our home, and then we'd take him back to the airport on Sunday. Most of that time, all we would do was sit at our kitchen table and talk about ideas for services and products we wanted to sell to our customers, or to the larger marketplace of people who had yet to do business with us.

We'd come up with some really cool ideas, drinking lots of coffee and just kicking back. We would always have a large stack of legal pads waiting for Russ, along with a bunch of pens, pencils, tape and scissors. That's as complicated as it got with him. We'd sit around the table, we'd talk about all these ideas and then, all of a sudden, Russ would get really excited and start writing. Then my wife Eileen and I would just shut up.

Russ would be writing furiously, really fast, turning the pages quickly. Sometimes he would be scribbling things out, sometimes he would be cutting and pasting. He would just go crazy for five or ten or fifteen minutes... then, all of a sudden, he would calm down. We'd pick up the coffee, we'd make him a pastry, we'd start talking, and he'd start reading back some of the stuff that he'd written. Then, all of a sudden, he'd get excited again, and he'd start writing fast and furious. Eileen and I would look at each other, and then we would watch this grown man get so excited. It was impressive and inspiring.

After we took him back to the airport, we would take those legal pads, have them typed up, do a little editing, and then we'd send those sales letters out—and money would come pouring in. I told myself, "Man, I have *got* to learn how to do this." **So I dedicated myself to that: I became passionate about becoming a good copywriter.** There's a lot to learn, but I was very, very hungry for it, and I learned a great deal from Russ.

Here's one of the most important things I learned. Although Russ did freelance copywriting, he also wrote copy for himself to develop his own products and services. **I'll never forget something he told me once: "T.J., you can always make more money writing copy for your own products and services than you'll ever make as a freelancer."** That advice has been worth millions of dollars to me.

Now, at one point, I wanted to be a freelance copywriter—and freelance copywriters do make huge sums of money. In fact, the demand is incredible, because every business needs more sales and more profits. When you tell a business owner, "I can make you more money," that's music to their ears. If you join our Get Paid to Write Coaching Program, you'll get our proven direct mail package that goes out to business owners offering them your freelance services. We've put together a tremendous direct mail package, and we'll tell you more about that later. First, though, I want you to think about this: **there are tens of millions of businesses here in America alone, and none of them are making enough sales and profits.** They always want to make more. This is a very lucrative proposition, for you *and* for them!

Of course, that doesn't mean that every single piece of copy that you write is going to make a profit; **there are a lot other things that go into a successful campaign in any business, and sometimes things don't work out as you hope they will.** But still, writing copy can be very lucrative, especially considered that it's based on things that you work on for just a few days—copy that's written once and edited to perfection during the creative process. If you're really sweating over a sales letter, it might take you a month or more, but in most cases that would be for a pretty extensive project. **The point is, the effort that you put in to create that one sales letter, or that one ad, can result in huge amounts of money coming in later on.**

Copywriting is Challenging

Let's move on to the third reason why I think you should consider copywriting as a career: it's challenging. I've been doing this for 23 years now, and that whole time, I've been committed to trying to become the very best copywriter I can possibly be. And it's not easy! There's always something new to learn. I've never woken up and thought, "Well, so much for copywriting. I've learned everything there is to learn." **There's plenty to do and plenty to learn, and I'm still trying to be the best I can be.** For example, in the last 30 days, I've written over 100,000 words of copy—sales copy, mostly. Over 100,000 words: that's as long as most novels. Now why have I done that? Am I insane? Not really (or at least, I hope not!). **No, I've done this to push myself, to sharpen my skills, to write more sales copy that'll produce more money for me and my company.**

Every hour you spend writing sales copy that you then send out to existing or prospective customers can make you tremendous amounts of money. There's no guarantee it will, but the potential is certainly there. This is challenging. **No matter how much you learn, there's always something *more* to learn.** And I'm sure that other areas of the writing field are the same way. I, personally, would be the world's worst fiction writer—seriously, a second-grade kid could write better fiction than me—but I've read enough on the subject to know that it's very much the same in that field, too. You could spend your whole life trying to become a good fiction writer and *still* not know it all. Writing sales copy is the same way.

Of course, business is somewhat challenging in and of itself. If it were easy, everybody would be doing it. So you also have the challenge that goes along with just being in business in general. **But with copywriting, the biggest challenge is in deciding which words are going to sell.** There's good copywriting and there's bad copywriting; sometimes it's easy to spot which is which, and sometimes it's not. **The challenge here comes in finding the right combination of words and story to present your case to your prospect so that they decide the money in their pocket is worth less than whatever it is you're promising to deliver to them.**

For example, if you're selling a cure for baldness, you'd better learn how to convince men who have no hair that the money you're charging for that cure is worth less than the cure. **The idea is to convince them to spend that money on the promise of a benefit.** You're promising them that if they'll give you $50 on this cure, then in six weeks they'll have hair on their heads again. If you choose the right words, that $50 is an easy exchange for them, because they want the benefits you're promising. **The real challenge, then, is in developing the ability to get people to see the worth in what you're offering.**

Copywriting is Creative

Last but not least, copywriting is a very creative way to make money. **In fact, it some ways it's just as creative as writing fiction.** Now, when most people dream of being a writer, what they really dream of is writing fiction, that Great American Novel. They want to be Stephen King or John Grisham. Part of the reason they want to write fiction is to tune into that creative center that's inside of all of us. They want to do artistic, work, where they can lose themselves in a great story. Well, I want to tell you this, and I'll repeat this throughout this book: **learning how to become a copywriter, or an information marketer, or a ghostwriter, is just as creative as writing fiction—and for most people, it's far more lucrative.** This is my solemn promise to you.

To be honest, I can't think of a worse way to make money than to try to write fiction. Now, I don't want to discourage you if that's your goal. You can always use one or all of our three methods of getting paid to write, and then write that novel on the side. If you want to write fiction, if that's your dream, at least you'll be getting paid to write; **but I promise you, learning how to become a copywriter, or using the other two methods that we have to get paid to write, can be absolutely creative and stimulating.** You never stop learning. You lose yourself in it, and you're only limited by your imagination. In many ways, it's just as creative as writing a novel. You come up with all kinds of ideas.

Every morning, my routine is this: I get up very early in the morning, and the first thing I do is jump in the shower... and I'll just sit in the shower until I get some ideas. (I have a special sit-down shower, if you were wondering). Very rarely do I know what I'm going to write the night before, though I do have my projects that I have to work on, usually large numbers of them. I just wait for the muse, the inspiration, to hit me. Sometimes I'll sit in there for 10 minutes; sometimes I'll sit in there for 30 minutes. And then all of a sudden a great idea comes, and I'll run downstairs and try to write 3,000 words as fast as I can. That's my goal every day.

Learning to write good sales copy is just as creative as writing that great American novel, and I want you to realize that. **A lot of people are looking for ways to express their creativity, and this is a wonderful way to do it.** You see, creativity is something that I think most people are born with, and they express it constantly at a very young age. Unfortunately, it fades as they get older. My Director of

Marketing, Chris Lakey, has six kids; and as I write this, his oldest daughter is 14. He tells me that she's not as creative as his four- or five-year-old children are. Little kids are *bursting* with creativity. They want to do creative things constantly; they need to have outlets for that creativity. Chris says that his little seven-year-old daughter is constantly coming up to him with pictures she's drawn. She's a very good artist, and she enjoys drawing.

As kids get older, their creativity shifts into other areas as they find the things that interest them the most. I believe a lot of times, our education system squelches that creativity; and that's why we end up losing some of it. But I think it's still there in most people, which is why you have adults getting into things that allow them to release their creative energy. **Writing is one of those creative outlets, and that's why blogging is popular. Writing sales copy can be another avenue for expressing yourself creatively, and you happen to get paid for it as well.** Writing sales copy can be a very enjoyable, creative process if you look at it that way. **And when you're making money with it, it usually doesn't become a bore.** What *does* become a bore is when you're not doing well with something, so that it gets tedious. Ah, but if you're doing it well, then the creativity that comes out through your writing can be fun, no matter what you're writing.

Chris Lakey started working for me 20 years ago, when he was 16. He didn't have to be around me for long before he caught the writing bug! I remember asking him about it way back then, and he was quite interested. It was the early days of the Internet, and he had a computer that his dad used for work. Well, Chris got to use it a little, and at first he just used it to chat with his friends in a precursor to instant messaging. Later, he started exploring this service called CompuServe. This was a new experience for Chris, because previously all his information had been served to him in textbooks, encyclopedias, and similar sources. But it wasn't really easily available. And now here was this Internet, which had all this information on a variety of things!

Things were a bit different back then; basically, you had to pay based on the information you wanted off the Internet. You couldn't just go to any website and download info, like you can do today. This was before the existence of the World Wide Web as we know it—so you paid for whatever you had access to. CompuServe came with a guide that listed the costs of various sites based on what they perceived the value was. They ranked websites like restaurant guides rank eateries; cheap information was one dollar sign, while more expensive information was ranked with two, three, or more.

When Chris was about 17, he found some information that he thought would be valuable for businesses, and decided to write his first sales copy. It was actually in brochure form, and he never did anything with it. Of course, his intent was to get the information off this new Internet thing, figuring that a lot of businesses didn't have access to it, or didn't know about it, or weren't as geeky as he was back then and wouldn't know how to find it—so it would be valuable to them. That was his first foray into writing sales copy, and he tells me that he's sure it was horrible. **It didn't come to much; but writing sales copy soon became one of his creative outlets, and it evolved into a profitable one.** After that first brochure, he kept writing, producing other copy, and gradually learned the craft—which brought him to where he is today!

Chapter Three:

Writing to the Audience

Here's an interesting story about Chris Lakey and his development as a sales writer, one that occurred about 10-12 years ago as I write this. He had some friends over to his house, and was showing them this sales letter that he had written. Chris was really proud of it, and thought he had done a good job. By then, he'd been writing copy for about 10 years as one of his creative outlets, and felt that he had some pretty good copywriting skills. His friends didn't really know a whole lot about the marketplace he was writing to, but nonetheless, he wanted them to know what he was up to, so he gave them a copy of his sales letter.

After flipping through it, they looked at him and said, "We don't understand this at all." Chris felt insulted, because he'd written what he thought was a really good sales letter, with well-done copy and a good offer. But his friends just didn't get the message. **Now, of course, he knows that the reason they didn't get it was that they weren't part of the marketplace he was writing to—so it didn't appeal or even make sense to them.** That sales letter went on to make Chris a pretty decent amount of money, because the market he was writing to *did* understand it, and they responded very well indeed.

One of the keys to successful copywriting is to make sure that you're writing to your proper audience; and to do

that, you need to know your audience very well. In this example, the people that Chris wrote his sales letter for completely got it, so the response was positive. When he showed it to people who weren't part of his target market, they didn't understand it. It was confusing to them. Of course they didn't buy; he wasn't *trying* to get them to buy. He just wanted them to see what he was doing, because he was justifiably proud of his work.

If you write a novel, you throw it out there, and you wait to see who's going to buy it. You may think about the marketplace a little first, but you're more likely to be thinking about what you want to say; you just hope that people like it and want to buy what you've written. **With writing sales copy, though, one of the top strategies is to start with your marketplace, and then write your sales message to that marketplace, knowing who they are and the kinds of things they respond to.** To me, that's the most important secret to becoming a great copywriter—simply to know your audience.

That leads me to a story of my own. When you study the subject of writing, you'll find that one of the things that everyone says is, **"Write what you know."** That's a general concept that applies to all aspects and subfields of writing, because your knowledge will come through if you do this. **Certainly, to be a great copywriter, you've got to know who you're writing to, and what they want:** what turns them on, what gets them excited. What benefits are most appealing to them? What offers have they bought before? **To discover all this, you have to study the marketplace closely.** That's a prerequisite, a reality that you can't work around, so never, ever forget it.

Within our first five years in business, we generated over $10 million in total revenue, and this was the number one secret that made us that money: we knew exactly who we were writing to. **We understood the market very well. The reason for that was simple: I *was* my marketplace.** I'd been buying from all of the companies we ultimately competed against... though the truth is, we weren't necessarily in business to compete against them. We were in business to make money for ourselves. I've paid very little attention to the competitors over the years, except to read their ads to keep track of certain general trends. **I certainly don't *worry* about competition.**

But as consumers in the marketplace, we understood exactly what people wanted, what they liked, what they didn't, what kinds of offers appealed to them, what kinds of benefits to express in our materials—and in general, what kinds of products and services to develop that they would go crazy over, that they would continue to buy again and again from us. As little kids like to taunt, **"It takes one to know one."** It really does.

And here's the thing: **when you're writing to someone you know a lot about, or when you're writing on a subject that you understand very well, you don't have to be that good in order to make a lot of money.** I want you to think deeply about that; just burn that idea into your mind. There's a great quote from the sixteenth century that goes, "In the land of the blind, the one-eyed man is king." I love that quote, because it epitomizes the principle I'm discussing here. If you know your market very well—who you're selling to, what they want, what turns them on more than anything else—and have all that down pat, then you don't have to be that good in order to make good money. I wasn't.

I still don't consider myself to a great writer... but **when it comes to writing to the people I sell to, I know exactly what they want, what they like, and what they dislike.** I'm hip to the kinds of offers they bite on, what they're looking for; and I know how to develop products and services to match those criteria, many of which are information related. **Basically, I've found a war that I can win.**

I already told you that there's no way on God's green Earth I'll ever be able to write fiction, no matter how bad I'd like to. I do read plenty of great fiction, and certainly I listen to books while I'm driving—and I'm well aware that the quality of writing is much greater than anything I'm capable of myself. It would be extremely intimidating for me to think that I could compete with those people. There's just no way. **And so I found a market I understand, a market I'm passionate about, a market that I actually enjoy.** By the way, a market is just a group of people who have something in common, something that causes them to buy certain products and services, something that causes them to pay attention to certain media—magazines, newspapers, TV, radio—where you can reach and target them. **You find prospective buyers by reaching into those niche markets.**

I feel that you need to take a page out of our playbook here, and find an area or a market that you can embrace. **Choose your market very carefully, because once you're in it, it's hard to get out of it.** Once you get established, the people who buy from you one time will buy from you again and again. **And of course, that's the secret to getting rich in all business: getting people to re-buy from you at a nice margin.**

CHAPTER FOUR:

Copywriting as a Business

Here's something that I feel I've got to get out of the way, now that I've outlined the basics of copywriting. I realize that many of you probably purchased our Get Paid to Write Program with absolutely, positively *zero* intention of ever being in any kind of business for yourself. You bought this program because you want to get paid to write! You don't want to be in business per se. **Well, if this is how you feel, then I want to express some ideas here in order to give you a little encouragement.**

First of all, you certainly *can* be a freelance copywriter— **but you have to realize that even then, you're still self-employed and therefore, in a very real sense, you own your own business.** Over time you develop your clientele, and you're able to spend most of your time writing copy for them... but you're still running a business. Now, I understand wholeheartedly if you just want to write and not worry about being in business. You see, that's me, too—even though I've been self-employed now since December 1985! I never really *wanted* to be self-employed; I just wanted the freedom that came with having my own company. I wanted to be able to call my own shots. I didn't want a boss breathing down my neck. I wanted to get out of the blue-collar work that I was doing. I was a welder, and before I was a welder I was a construction worker. Before that, I worked in the oil fields... and I didn't want to do that kind of work for the rest of my life. I especially didn't want to have to take crap off somebody who told me what to do all day long.

The bottom line is, I still don't consider myself to be a businessperson in a traditional sense. **I'm an entrepreneur. I'm a marketer. I'm a copywriter. I've been fortunate in that I've always had others who helped me run the business, starting with my wife Eileen, who ran the company for the first 14 years.** That freed me up to spend all my time learning how to become a copywriter, learning how to develop informational products, working with ghostwriters, and doing the kinds of things I'll talk about throughout this book.

Even though Eileen ultimately had to step down due to health reasons and **I've had the company now for almost 10 years, I** *still* **have other people running the company for me.** These are people who are talented at what they do—just like Eileen, who was super-talented at what she did. They do a great job. **I hire good people and leave them alone to do what they do best, while I do what** *I* **do best.** I spend the majority of my time sitting on my rear dreaming up new ideas, coming up with all kinds of creative projects for products and services—and constantly writing the sales materials that cause people to take the actions that we want them to take, to give their money to us. **I still do that to this day. Other people run the company.**

Chris Lakey is another good example. When Eileen stepped down as President and CEO of our company and I took over that slot, Chris stepped into my slot as Marketing Director. He spends the majority of his time writing, too. So think about that. **Yes, we have a business, and I'm sure that some of you didn't purchase this program to have anything to do with being self-employed** *or* **having a business.** You've always been told all kinds of negative things about being in business for yourself, I'd imagine. But the truth is that in some cases, you've simply been told wrong.

I'm here to tell you that you can structure your business so that other people take care of all the paperwork and the other necessary day-to-day things that, frankly, just bore the crap out of me. I know that Chris feels the same way, and you probably do too! **Well, you can delegate all the boring but necessary things, leaving you to spend the majority of your time writing.** So don't be close-minded to the idea of making a business of writing.

When you get right down to the basics, a business is pretty simple anyway... although I'll admit that it *can* get pretty complicated at times, especially when you start running low on cash. Otherwise, I like to think of it as a simple machine—like one of those old fashion watches that works using a series of cogs and gears. Your employees and team members are those cogs and gears. **You have different people who assume different responsibilities in the framework of your business machine, which gives you time to do what you do best— which is getting paid to write.**

What Do You Know?

As I discussed in the previous chapter, the best way to make money with copywriting is to write about something you know well. Therefore, **the best way to succeed in the copywriting business is to sell to a marketplace that you're very familiar with.** Here's an example: if you happen to be a good golfer and you've discovered a golfing secret that, when used, shaves ten strokes off the average game and will help you win more tournaments, you can start by writing about that. **You can actually sell your strategy, then go from there to create all kinds of money-making opportunities based on the point-shaving strategies you've discovered.** You can use your experience to create a valuable information product that people will be eager to buy.

Information publishing is one of the easiest ways to get into copywriting—especially on the Internet, where it's a piece of cake to deliver products for free. Publishing your information in digital format and then selling it via a website is a good, easy way to get started. But however you decide to package and deliver it, start by writing about things that you know the most about. **Create information that has value, and then write copy to sell that information to other people.**

In the golfing industry, that might be a golf tip; maybe you've got that special strategy I mentioned earlier for lowering your golf score, or perhaps you've discovered the ultimate set of golf clubs—or you've had your own golf clubs designed, based on your own experience. Maybe you've discovered this special club that hits the ball farther or straighter, or a putter that allows greater precision. **Just take what you know and create information that shares that with others.**

You're the expert here: most people simple don't know all that you know about whatever you're writing about, particularly when you're focused on something specialized. **With your information product, you can educate them—and it doesn't necessarily take a whole lot of knowledge above and beyond the average to write up information that other people would find valuable.** Golfing, just to go back to that as an example, is a huge industry—and you already know that people are spending millions if not billions of dollars on it every year. The market for golf improvement products is simply enormous. Mailing lists exist, magazines exist, websites exist, that target those buyers—and those people do spend a lot of money trying to improve their game. It's a fairly insatiable marketplace, in fact, because no one really ever masters the techniques they teach you, so there's always a demand for more information.

Fishing is another huge industry. People never catch big enough fish often enough, and they're always in the market for more products—fishing reels, rods, baits, lures, and gimmicks— that will help them catch fish. If you happen to be an avid fisherman, there may be ways for you to enter that marketplace and sell your product, your service, your information by writing attractive sales copy to your fellow fishermen.

Whatever it is, if you start with something you know, something you're passionate about, writing copy is really just a transfer of emotion. In fact, that's what *all* selling is. If I'm excited about something and I can get *you* excited about it, I might be able to get you to spend money because of that excitement. If I've got a secret that's making me hit the golf ball farther and I'm excited about that, and I tell you how excited I am and how much it's improved my game, you're more likely to spend $25 or $50 on it if you think it will work. **That's really what it's all about: transferring emotion from the person selling the product or service to a person looking to receive the benefits of that information.**

You *Are* the Business

I know that many of you reading this probably don't want a business. Honestly, I don't know a whole lot of people who necessarily like the idea, especially if they're familiar with all that's involved. I'll be the first one to admit that there are a *lot* of hassles and headaches that go with having a business. There are taxes to be paid, there are employees to be supported, there are regulations that have to be followed, and there are customers to be dealt with—and that's just a few of the things you face as a business owner. **There are all kinds of challenges that go into having a successful and profitable business, and most people don't want to undergo those.**

Yet all that's part and parcel of the business life, which is why, if the whole idea turns you off, I've suggested that you get around some of that less-than-glamorous stuff by using other people to help you in those areas. Again, I think I'm a perfect example of that. I'm first and foremost an entrepreneur and a writer, and yet I have a company—so I hire people to carry out the other tasks related to the business, so I can do what I do best and what I enjoy doing most. **You can do that in your business, too. A lot of people do it very successfully.** Even writers of fiction and non-fiction who work alone will often set up their own companies, because of tax and accounting benefits. They arrange it so they don't get paid directly as an individual, and have people who handle their accounting.

Don't think about business as a bad thing... though it's a necessary evil, if you want to look at it that way. It's something that helps you in the long run, and it usually sets you up to be more profitable because of accounting laws, taxes, and other government-related garbage I don't even want to get into here. Just know that business is not a four-letter word, and it's not something to be scared of. **It can be an asset. And in any case, there are things you can do to reduce the burden of having a**

business, so you can stick to your writing without having to worry too much about everything else.

Copywriting is a great business to be in. **It can be amazingly lucrative, fun, creative, and challenging**—and the truth is you don't have to be the best copywriter in the world as long as you're in a market that you know well, that you're passionate about, and you're selling to people who have the same interest you have. **It's a great lifestyle when you can throw yourself wholeheartedly into a market that already interests you.** Build your business around it, with all the other specialists who can help you do the job effectively, and you'll be able to spend the majority of your time writing about things that are a part of you and very personal to you.

I've been writing copy for 23 years. I'm still learning—but during all those years, I was getting paid a high six-figure income every year, even while I was refining my skills. **It's great to be able to get paid so handsomely even while you're learning!** That's one of the most encouraging things about copywriting, if you ask me. So just stay open and receptive to the self-employment part of it. **Even if you don't want to have your own company, realize that it's advantageous to do so, because you need those benefits of being in business.**

If you arrange things properly, you can write all the time without worrying too much about the business, while enjoying all the wonderful income and freedom that being in business can bring.

The Money Part of Copywriting

In this chapter, I'll outline the profitable foundation of copywriting. I suspect that this is the one thing that will get you the most excited about the prospect of becoming a copywriter, and will make you much more willing to take the time and make the effort necessary to learn how to become a good copywriter. You see, I've been there myself.

In the beginning, I never really wanted to be a copywriter, or get into the information marketing business, or learn about ghostwriting. I didn't want to do *any* of that. **I just wanted to be a millionaire!** All I cared about was making money. **But somewhere along the line, I fell in love with copywriting and information marketing, and now I do it for more reasons than just making money.** And yet, the money... it's just so astronomical. The amount of money that you can potentially make—and I guarantee you can, because I have—is so astounding that I thought I'd start out here by giving you some examples, to hopefully get you even more thrilled about this.

We've had many sales letters that have generated over a million dollars in profit. These are letters that we've written ourselves, not paid a freelance copywriter to write for us. You know, when you have the ability to put words on paper, or on a website, or in a magazine ad that causes thousands of people to send you their money, **it's one of the most thrilling**

experiences possible. Some people say it's better than sex, but I'll leave it to you to decide that! **The point is, it's an amazing feeling—and it's something that you *can* experience.** But it does take some time and effort to learn how to do this.

The first sales letter that I ever wrote that made us over a million dollars took me three months to write—three months of slaving over that letter every single day. **I questioned myself about every single word.** And back then, I didn't write on the computer at all: I did it all with legal pads. I still have that sales letter. In fact, it's a little embarrassing for me to look at the way I wrote it back then because, believe it or not, I wrote it all longhand... and then I taped all of the pages together.

It was wrapped up like a great big toilet paper roll. I would go through it and read it carefully, word by word, and every time I saw a place that had to be edited, I would bring out the scissors, cut it, and insert the new copy in there. It sounds so ridiculous now! And of course, it was very time consuming. **I was careful and meticulous; I rewrote it, and rewrote it, and rewrote it, a million times it seems.** It took me three months to do it, and it was just a 24 page sales letter. **But it was worth it! A few months after we put it out there, that one letter had generated over a million dollars**—and it was such a simple idea that I was selling.

Now, some people would say that three months to work on one letter is a long time. And certainly, we do that kind of thing now in a week to 10 days; and it's all on computers. No more giant scrolls! **We've been doing it a long time now, so it's easier and quicker. But even if it weren't, even if it still took months of unremitting labor to write a profitable letter...** well, consider this. Some authors will spend years writing a much longer book that doesn't generate nearly as much money. Year after year, they work on the same piece of writing. In comparison to that, even if it took us three months to write a letter, it would be well worth it! Of course, it doesn't anymore; we're prolific and experienced enough to produce high quality copy in a short period of time.

These days, Chris Lake is my co-writer on all of our sales material. **Sometimes he takes the lead and starts the letter, and then I work on it; sometimes vice versa. Either way, that gives us the synergistic power of working together.** Just a word to the wise: having people to work with is a valuable thing. For maybe six or seven years, we wrote sales letters with a group of other people who were in our same business. Again, it was usually Chris and I that would start these letters; but then, the group would get on the phone for a couple hours a week, and we would go over these letters line by line. The group actually made recommendations that made those letters super-strong. Plus, it was a great learning experience! At one time, there were as many as 10-12 of us who were producing these sales letters and other enclosures for our sales material. **Having a team of other writers to work with is something that I think you should definitely consider, because you end up with all these different ideas from the various minds involved.** This is something that's helped us a great deal.

A good example is a project that we're involved in right here and right now, at the time of this writing. This is a project that started with a joint venture partner in Florida, a man who wrote a sales letter and wanted to send it out to a small group of our clients whom he thought would be interested in this particular opportunity he has. **He wrote the letter and we**

**endorsed it, which simply means that we included a cover
letter along with his sales materials that was from me,
though I didn't write it.**

This is a partner that we've had a good long relationship
with. I didn't even see the letter that he wrote that had my name
and picture on it. But it didn't matter; I trust the man. He's a
good friend of ours. We're doing business with someone we can
count on. All I did was have our mailing house make names
available to him, and then they mailed the letters out. He paid
for everything; we didn't pay one single penny. And, so far, in a
very fast period of time, we've generated almost $100,000 in
profit *just* from the sales letter that he wrote on this opportunity
that he stumbled on to and developed himself. Well now, all of a
sudden we're excited! **Making $100,000 very quickly without
doing anything at all is enough to get anybody excited.
Therefore, we're developing our own sales material on the
same general subject.**

I just thought I'd tell you just a little bit about how we do it.
Hopefully, it'll inspire you to create your own project!

I started on this yesterday morning. Now, my goal is to
write 2,740 words a day; but I always try to write a little more
than that. And so, yesterday, as part of my daily writing
commitment, I wrote 3,700 words on the new project. That was
my very first day. Today was my second day, and I wrote 3,500
words on that project. I'm doing this in a multi-step process
where I don't even worry about paragraph breaks or even,
necessarily, about spelling correctly—although I try to do my
best, so I don't have to go back and clean it up. **The thing is,
when I get on a roll, I start trying to type faster than I
actually can... or at least, the words start coming through me**

faster than I can type. My goal is to just get as many words out there as fast as I can.

This is a tip that I learned from my favorite musician, Neil Young—a man who's so amazing prolific that he's written probably five or six hundred songs. As he pointed out once, **"When you think, you stink. You just let it come out." So that's how I write my sales material, and for the moment, all I'm doing is focusing on the benefits.** I've gotten all the sales materials that our friend in Florida put together. Plus, there are a lot of other people promoting this particular opportunity on the Internet, so I've got their material to use as research. I went to all these websites and printed out all the good sales material... of which there is very little, by the way. That's the most amazing thing about this! There are literally hundreds of other people involved in the very same opportunity who have websites... and although I spent an hour yesterday morning looking for good copy, I found very little of it.

In a way, that's exciting. I was looking for ideas that I could review and expand upon, and **there's very little decent sales copy out there. Why is that a good thing? Because it means that people are making good money with lousy copy, so imagine the profit potential if you can write great copy! That's pretty exciting to me.** So anyway, I gathered up all this material, I reviewed it thoroughly, and then yesterday morning I started writing as fast and as furious as I could. I wrote as much as I could on every benefit that this particular opportunity offers. **I got into the zone—and I only write during peak moments, by the way, in the morning when my energy is very good.** If I try to do it in the afternoon, my writing sucks. Sometimes in the evening, when I'm really tired, I can get on a roll; but not often.

There's a peak writing time for each of us. For some people, it's early morning; for a lot of people, it's late in the evening. **It's up to you to discover when your peak time is.** You need to experiment until you can find a time when you can just focus and zone out—when you can get into this rhythm where it all becomes easier. All I try to do is get as many words out there as fast as I can. This morning, after I took a little break, I took a shower, came downstairs, and I had a little bit of time left to go—so I decided to see how much I could do. I wrote 1,244 words in 27 minutes. I got on a roll; I just zoned out and wrote as fast as possible.

Of course, this kind of "speed-writing" comes with experience. **You have to know the benefits that your audience is looking for, and you have to be able to fall into the zone at will.** I'm not going to mislead you here; it does take time to learn all that. But once you've got it down, when you know what the people you're writing this copy to are interested in and which benefits appeal to them, and you've done enough of it... then you don't want to think at all. **You just want to let it come out as fast as possible.**

And the writing has an edge to it. **You'll still have to go back and clean it up; you'll have to cut certain sentences out, and you may have to cut full paragraphs out.** You may even have to cut whole *pages* out. But still, it tends to be edgy and sharp, speaking directly to the heart of the prospect. I'll spend four or five days just doing what I call brain dumping: writing as fast as I can about every possible benefit, just trying to see how many words I can put out there. On the second day, I'm coming up with ideas I didn't have on the first day. By the fourth day, I'm really familiar with the subject—and a lot of times, that's when I produce my best copy. I'll often throw away the stuff that I did on the first day, or hardly use any of it. **But in the end, the copy is alive; it's got energy to it.**

Once I've put together the copy, I'll start editing it down. That's the kind of work I can do at nighttime in front of the TV with my wife. I've got the laptop in my lap, and it's quiet. **I don't need that same level of intensity when I do my editing.** The rewriting is actually a lot of fun sometimes, because you *can* take your time and do it while you're doing other things—for example, while you're watching football or baseball. You can't do it while you're watching basketball, of course, because you can't take your eyes off the TV for too long with basketball!

But you get my point. In any case, **I'll spend several days reworking what I've written into a sales letter, using only the best copy, and doing a little rewriting and reformatting. Then I'll give it to Chris Lakey, and let him smooth it out and edit it and add his two cents.** Within ten days from the time I started, which was yesterday, we'll have a sales letter that's just as good as, if not even better than, the original letter that was written by and belongs to our partner in Florida.

Our letter could generate hundreds of thousands or, potentially, even millions of dollars—all for ten days of work. And even when the promotion is over, it doesn't just stop there. **We'll take that big block of sales copy, along with anything that wasn't used in the original sales materials, and create a series of sequential follow-up mailings to go out to the people who initially requested the free information package from us.** It's a two-step approach. The first step is that we'll offer a report, or maybe Chris and I will record a CD about the biggest benefits that are outlined in the sales material. People request this low-cost or no-cost item, and then in the second step (which can be quite involved), we go after those leads with the initial package we send out and then a series of follow-up mailings. **We're extremely relentless about the way that we follow up.** We'll create many different follow-up letters; in some extreme cases, as many as 20. Each will be small chips from the big block of copy that was initially written and refined over a ten-day period.

Let me re-emphasize this point: **the more you can focus on the people you're writing to and the main benefits, the better. Because that's what people buy: the main benefits of your offer.** So while you're writing, just let it all out; don't try to do any kind of editing. Don't try to second-guess yourself. Know that you may have to throw away half of it. Who cares? It's liberating. There's a freedom that comes from pulling out all the stops and filters, just writing like crazy and not even worrying about what's good, what's bad, what you're going to use, and what you're not. Simply determine how many words you're going to write, how much time you're going to spend on it, or a certain number of pages you'd like to complete — whatever. Then try to do all you can over a set period of time, whether it's four or five days or four or five weeks.

When you're first getting started, remember my story. My first real sales letter took me three months. Now, had I known what I do now, I could have done it in much less time; but the point is, I was just learning back then. Yet I was second guessing myself every step of the way, and I just refuse to do that nowadays. The editing comes later. The rewriting comes later. And when you do rewrite, I guarantee you'll come up with more ideas, just from looking at your copy. **Some of your best ideas, in fact, will actually come in the editing stage, when you're more familiar with the material.** You're more comfortable with it, and you have time to see what you actually wrote. **Now, you're able to judge it a little (because you're not judging on the first step at all), and then you're able to come up with ideas that strengthen and solidify it.**

Look, this is fun. It's exciting. When you're doing this, whether you're working freelance or selling your own stuff, it's still exciting. **It's the thrill of the chase, the joy of the hunt.** It's fueled by the challenge of it all, the game of it. **It really, truly is thrilling, and as with all good sports, you can win big.** As our friend, Russ von Hoelscher, once told me, "All it takes is one well-executed idea to make a million dollars," and he couldn't have been more right about that. **The fact that you can take a week or two weeks or two months of your time and create something that generates hundreds of thousands or millions of dollars in total revenue is very, very exciting.** It's worth learning how to do for that reason alone. If you still want to do other kinds of writing, then you can do that on the side—but this is writing that really does pay off.

The Swipe File Concept

Here's another recommendation, one that's helped me make millions: keep a swipe file of good sales material. That is, **when you find something that really speaks to you, copy it or print it out, and put it in a file so that you can refer to it later, using it as a model for your own work.** This requires that you read a lot of sales material in every venue available, so you'll know the difference between good and bad. The more you study it, the more you'll realize just how much bad copy is out there. There are so many people out there writing sales copy who don't know what the hell they're doing—and so the copy is just lousy. It doesn't do a good job of convincing people of anything, so its sales potential is poor. You'll start to see this if you read enough sales copy; **it won't be long before you'll be able to instantly recognize the difference between good sales copy and bad sales copy.**

Good sales copy sticks with you, like a good song. I've got songs in my head right now from some of my favorite musicians; they just keep playing in my mind over and over again, because these songs have a certain hook to them. There's something I identify with in those songs; something that keeps them locked in my head. Good sales copy has the same kind of hook—and the more you read other people's copy, the more you'll see that. **When you buy our program, we'll include our favorite swipe file, to help you see the difference. That way, you can study good, profitable copy.**

To Be a Copywriter

So what does it mean to be a copywriter? Well, there are a lot of different angles that you can take, and I think I've made a good start so far in this book; but trying to condense them down into any specific format is a daunting task. The task of becoming a good copywriter isn't something that's easily learned over a short period of time. I think if you talk to any copywriter, no matter whether they're freelancers or write for themselves, **they'll tell you that they haven't learned everything yet; no matter how experienced they are, they've never completely mastered copyrighting.** Oh, they may be really good at it, but they would never tell you that they've learned everything there is to learn about writing great sales copy, because **there are always new things to learn.**

Someone who wrote good sales copy 20 years ago might have been good before the Internet came around, but if they want to be a good Internet copywriter, then there are some new things to learn—not the core strategies, but **the basic methods that you use to reach people on the Internet, which are a little bit different than they are for traditional sales copy.** There's *always* something new on the horizon. There's always a new technique to master or a new strategy to pick up on. People are always innovating.

Just as an artist admires another artist or a sports figure admires other athletes, copywriters admire each other's work. It's not uncommon to come across a sales letter that someone else has written and to be impressed by it, to see something you like, and to want to model a new offer that you're doing after something you see someone else doing. This is where swipe files become invaluable. **One of the important ways that you can stay up on what's happening in the world of copyrighting is to see what other people are writing about and the style and words that they're using to capture the interests and the imaginations of their readers, and to keep track of it all.** You can easily collect multiple file cabinets full of great ads and sales letters.

In fact, it's important that you become a student of the techniques that other people are using to sell their products and services. Now, it can get daunting at times, when you have tons of these sales letters and ads to deal with—and there are different strategies that people use for that. Some people keep full sales letters; others cut out the parts of the letter that interest them the most and toss the rest. Maybe they cut out headlines, and keep a folder full of those, so that any time they have a need of a great headline, they'll go to their headline swipe file and scan through it. They'll pick one that looks good, and maybe it works for what they're trying to do. They'll rewrite it a little bit, and they've got a new headline. **A swipe file is a really important aspect of being a good copywriting student.**

Of course, there are formulas that people use to write, like AIDA: Attention, Interest, Desire, Action. I've talked about copyrighting formulas for success before. Always make sure you capture people's attention; then make sure you get their interest, build the desire, and then make a call to action. **If you'll just do those things, your sales letter can be super-successful.** And sure, those simple formulas are important; but if all you're doing is writing the formula, without really understanding who you're writing to, your formula is only going to take you so far.

Here's a word of caution I'd like to throw out quickly while I'm thinking about it. There are many, many information products out there. You can do a search on the Internet for "copywriting strategies" or "copywriting success" or something similar, and you'll get lots of hits from people selling information about writing sales copy. **But you need to be careful about two things: what they're doing to write sales copy themselves, and how successful they've been using their own strategies.** A lot of the information you'll find can be useful, and it can help you get ahead—but you need to be careful who you're listening to. That's critical. You absolutely need to find out if the strategies, suggestions, and tips you're getting are coming from people who have actually made money doing the things they're teaching you how to do.

There's a lot of bad information out there, especially in the way of free information. A lot of these websites and blogs will in fact teach you how to do something... but sadly, you're getting what you've paid for. If someone's willing to teach you their strategies for free, you always want to be leery of what they're teaching. Have they had success with it? If so, why are they passing it on for free? **Is that free information a marketing tool? Ironically, that usually makes it more legitimate!** Certainly, there are instances where someone is teaching you something for free as an introduction to a coaching program or something like it, where you *can* get valuable, useful information, because they're trying to sell you something else.

Just be careful on the Internet, because a lot of information available out there isn't necessarily being offered by people who have successfully used their own strategies, and haven't had a successful business in copywriting. **You never have to worry about that with our Get Paid To Write program.** You know our stuff works, because we've made millions doing this! I'm mentioned before that our company has been in business since 1988, mostly based on sales letters that have been written by us. Oh, in some instances we've joint ventured with people or used sales letters that weren't written by us to bring in money; but you can bet we carefully vetted that sales material before we ever committed ourselves. **The truth is, for most of those years, the sales letters that *we* have written have been responsible for bringing in the money that we've made.** Since 1988 we've brought in well over $110 million in sales, selling products and services to our marketplace *using sales copy that was written by us*. That's where all the tips, the stories that we offer from our own experiences, come in handy. **We know very well the strategies and systems required for writing sales copy that sells.**

Earlier, I outlined the project we're working on right now; that's a great example of how sales copy is written, at least at M.O.R.E., Inc. There are a lot of similar examples stretching back over our 23-year history. Here's one: back in the early 1990s, people started figuring out how to make money with computer bulletin boards, a kind of precursor to the World Wide Web. We thought this was an excellent opportunity—so we took the information we had, built a product around it to show our clients how to make money on computer bulletin boards, and created a sales letter to send out to people we thought would be interested. That sales letter brought in huge amounts of money. Orders were just flooding in; phones were ringing off the hook; fax machines were going crazy. The mail was piling high with orders for people wanting the information that we had compiled on how to make money with these computer bulletin boards.

I spent some time writing that sales letter, and in the end, it was worth probably a million dollars or more. It was a hugely successful promotion, with an enormous return on investment! **Later, in the late 1990s, we tackled what we called "Internet real estate"—domain names.** We wrote a sales letter showing people how they could make money with domain name speculation. If you remember, back in the late 1990s, people were buying up domain names like crazy, and some of them were being sold for millions of dollars. We taught our clients how to do that.

Now, those are just two profitable examples I can think of, going back to the 1990s. In the 2000s, we had a lot of similar

success stories. There are times when things don't work out as
well, of course, so we have an equal number of failures that we
could share with you—**and there's probably plenty you could
learn from us sharing our negative results as well. But the
point is that the successful sales letters we've written over
the years have produced tens of millions of dollars in sales.**
Individually, some produced a few tens of thousands, some
hundreds of thousands, and some millions.

Before I move on, I want to share something interesting
with you. People always wonder about the value of a sales letter.
What's it worth? That's an excellent question. I've told you that
some of our money was made with sales letters that we didn't
write. **Well, one example of that was a sales letter that sold a
package of products that we *knew* was successful in our
marketplace, because it had worked like gangbusters for the
company that was using it.** The gentleman who wrote the sales
letter was a business associate of ours. We had some experience
with him, and considered him a friend in business. We knew
about this super-successful sales letter that he had written and
knew that we could make a lot of money with it as well... we
just needed to be able to get permission to use his letter. But
instead of joint venturing with him, where we would have had to
give up a percentage and split the money, we wanted to keep all
the money. **We wanted to use his letter and be able to sell it to
our customers.** We worked out an agreement to do that, and I
believe the total money we paid him was $125,000.

**Now, that was for more than the sales letter: we
actually ended up getting all his product fulfillment
materials, and the rights to everything else that was a part
of that package.** But what we really wanted were the rights to

that killer sales letter, because it was super-successful. Now, many people thought that we were completely crazy for paying him $125,000 for that! In fact, even some people within our own staff thought that Eileen and I had gone off the deep end and that this was a completely stupid decision, basically throwing money down the drain. They kept telling us that it was probably the worst decision we could ever have made... and yet the decision was made.

We kept mailing that sales letter and selling that product for years—so in the end, the critics were wrong. I don't have the numbers here in front of me, but it wouldn't surprise me if that promotion made well over a million dollars. **In fact, we got double value out if it, because at one point it was our control piece**—that is, the item we were mailing to brand new customers on a regular weekly basis to bring them into the fold. That's how successful it was, because you send people who haven't worked with you before only the very best you have to offer. **So it was a wildly successful promotion that brought back probably over ten times the amount that was paid to license that letter.** We used someone's sales letter, so in essence that made this gentleman a copywriter for hire. I think this is an excellent example of purchasing copywriting services from someone else, though in that case he didn't write it with the intent of it being a letter that he sold.

A Famous Copywriting Example

Although I've cautioned you about depending on some of the copywriting teachers you'll find on the Internet, this venue does offer access to some incredible examples of sales copy that you can use as models and keep in your swipe file. **For**

example, one of the most (if not *the* most), successful sales letters of all time generated an estimated $2 billion in revenue for the *Wall Street Journal*. You can find that one online if you look; most copywriters have seen some version of this letter before in some format, because it's famous in the field. It's just a short, two-page sales letter that sells the *Wall Street Journal*, essentially to young business professionals. It includes a lot of the formulas and key ingredients that are important to formulating a good sales letter.

It starts out with a story set on a beautiful late spring afternoon 25 years ago, when two young men graduate from the same college. They're very much alike. But when these same two men return for their 25th reunion, their stories are quite different. One is wildly successful; one is not. What's the difference? **What makes one guy super successful and another guy an average Joe? Simply what each person knows, and how he or she makes use of that knowledge.**

Then the ad starts discussing the *Wall Street Journal*: how it's a publication like no other, and how knowledge is power; and it points out that the knowledge you get by being a subscriber to the *Wall Street Journal* is invaluable, and will help you be the guy who goes to his 25th reunion and is super-successful. Next, they make you a great introductory offer: at the time, you could subscribe for $28 and get 13 weeks of the *Journal*. It calls that offer an investment in success, because of all the useful knowledge in the *Journal* that will help you succeed. It even ends with a P.S. that says it's important to note that the subscription price may be tax deductible; so they're telling the reader, "Hey, you can even write it off on your taxes — what could be better than that?"

This was a great sales letter that was mailed for a long time. **It was probably the most successful sales letter ever, and as such offers an excellent model for any copywriter—and in fact, it's one that thousands have used.** There are many such examples you can look to, and you can even find this one on websites today, though it's no longer used by the *Journal* and hasn't been sent to anyone in years.

Here's something interesting, something that makes me laugh: when I found a website containing this sales letter, I noticed that all kinds of people had commented on it... and a lot of them talked about how this letter just isn't very good. It's only two pages, they say. It's kind of boring. They're dogging on it and criticizing all aspects of it, thinking that this little letter *surely* isn't the greatest sales letter of all time. One person commenting said that they didn't understand why this letter was so successful. But here's the thing: it was. There's no doubting that. Maybe the market has changed somewhat since it was used last, but it obviously spoke to the target market, and I suspect that if it were modified a bit, it still would. This is based on something that a lot of would-be copywriters just have trouble getting through their heads: *it was written precisely to its target market.* **That's the basis of all successful copywriting.** Not everyone is going to look at it and be moved by it, especially if it wasn't written for them. Not every copywriter is going to like the letter or even think it's very well-written. But it was aimed precisely toward the marketplace it was trying to reach, and it did a very good job of selling what it was trying to sell. That's all that really matters.

This *Wall Street Journal* letter was written to people in their college years who were getting ready to figure out what they were going to do with their lives. That story of the two graduates meeting again 25 years later, and their success or lack thereof being based on a decision made decades earlier, no doubt had a significant effect on the target market. The difference, though they don't say it, was apparently that one of them subscribed to the *Wall Street Journal* and one did not. **That's the implication here, and they do point out that knowledge is power. So they're reaching their target audience with the right message at the right time through the right medium.** That was part of what made their campaign so successful, even though some people look at that piece of copy now and say, "There's nothing special about that letter."

The important part of copywriting is not necessarily writing skill, because you can write a really good sales letter and have it bomb if it doesn't reach the right marketplace. I've said it before, and I'll probably say it again before I'm through: **first and foremost, it's critical to know who you're selling to, the marketplace that you're trying to reach. From there, you can figure out how to write a good sales letter to that marketplace.** Your sales letter doesn't have to be deathless prose. It doesn't have to be formatted just right. It doesn't even have to follow all of the copywriting rules. But if you understand your marketplace, and you have passion and enthusiasm for the product or service you're selling, then you can write good sales copy to that marketplace even before you know all the rules, even before you've studied all the formulas, even before you've built a big swipe file.

Choose your marketplace carefully, and learn everything you can about it. This is especially important if you're writing copy for your own products and services.

Subscribe to all the relevant newsletters and papers. Be a buyer of other products, services, and information in that marketplace. **Endeavor to know your customers and prospects inside and out—better than they know themselves.** That will be the foundation for you learning how to write effective sales copy that speaks to that marketplace. If you're a freelance copywriter, then whenever you get hired for a specific job, you need to work toward understanding the marketplace you're writing to.

I would say that it's also important for you to be well-read in general, especially on non-fiction topics. **Be up on the news, current trends, and fads—because you never know what your next job is going to have you writing about.** You never know when you're going to need a good story, and you never know when you're going to require information about a certain subject area. Knowing what's going on in the world, in sports, politics, health, and just about everything, will be useful just because you'll know more about a lot of different things— and you'll be able to incorporate some of those stories and facts into your copy.

And then, of course, you have to learn more specifically about the marketplace that you're writing to. **In-depth knowledge of the marketplace is the precursor, the constant in all copywriting equations.** The copywriting formulas and the strategies that you use are all very important, and you should know them. But if you know the marketplace first and foremost, and if you're good at understanding your customers or your average prospect and what they want, then that's how you come around to knowing what benefits they want the most, knowing what triggers they respond to emotionally. You'll be able to write better sales copy just because you have a better understanding of your market place. **So start with the marketplace first; the copywriting can come second.**

It's all about salesmanship, really. And yes, I realize that when you bought a program called "Get Paid to Write," you probably had no intention of becoming a salesperson. But consider this: **the two things that all selling really boils down to are influence and persuasion.** And here's a cool thing: in this kind of salesmanship, where you reach out and touch people through direct mail or advertisements in the media, you only hear the yeses. **You never hear the nos, so you have zero rejection!** People who don't care what you have to offer simply aren't going to respond at all.

You can't forget, either as a copywriter or as an individual, that a good copywriter (especially a good direct response copywriter) is a salesperson. They're trying to sell you. **They're trying to convince you that what they have to offer is worth more than the money they're asking for in return.** I love the example of the *Wall Street Journal* letter I discussed earlier, because that two page letter generated a couple of *billion* dollars in sales. And here's the clincher: over the years, many, many freelance copywriters have tried to beat that letter, and they just couldn't do it. Truly, as the commenters on that website pointed out, it's not that impressive a letter... but it tells a very persuasive story. Everybody wants to be the guy that succeeded, so it's a very effective example of the before and after story form. People always want to be the after, not the before. **They want the benefits. They want the results... and they want some secret to get those results, something really simple and easy.** Well, what could be simpler and easier than subscribing to the *Wall Street Journal?* Just give that company your money, and boom!

You're going to be the one who succeeded. That's persuasive.

Getting to people this way doesn't require you to be the greatest writer ever. If it took great writing skill, there's no way that I would be a copywriter, I can tell you that! As I mentioned in an earlier chapter, my writing, isn't that good. But I do know the customers in my marketplace. I know the benefits they want, and I know that they'll continue to buy those same benefits over and over again. **So to succeed, you just have to become very well-versed in knowing what people want and don't want, and the main objections you need to overcome.**

And basically, when you stay in the same marketplace, you're writing the same sales letter over and over. We've written thousands of different sales letters for the marketplace we serve—but while they were for different promotions, they were all basically the same. Sure, there are always unique aspects; but there are plenty of similarities too, because again, it's the benefits that people want. **The end emotional result that people are looking for: that's what a benefit is. It's all about persuasion.**

Cautionary Tales

I'd like to relate a few quick stories here that will hopefully stick in your mind, to emphasize a few of the lessons I've learned about copywriting over the years.

For the first eight years of our company, we hired freelancers to help us with our promotions; we had at least half a dozen different freelance copywriters that we paid money to. And I'll never forget this one guy I found who was advertising in the *DM News*. He still has his ad in there, every issue. Well, I paid him $8,000, and he flew in from Florida. We live an hour from the airport, so I drive him home from Wichita. I'd just met the guy, and yet he starts bragging to me about all the money he's making off all his clients—about how he's has these clients who have paid him hundreds of thousands of dollars. He just goes on and on, incessantly bragging.

I came very close to turning the car around and taking him back to the airport; I had to exercise some major impulse control not to. **It was immediately obvious that this guy was going to try to milk me for all I was worth;** that's basically what he was telling me with his story. **That's proof, though, that there's a tremendous demand out there for freelance copywriters;** otherwise, he wouldn't be making so much off his clients. I sat there and listened to him natter on about all this money he's making from all his clients for the first 10-15 minutes of the drive! And while that is, in fact, proof of the profitability of this field, evidence of tremendous need for freelance copywriters, what it did was inspire me to *not* want to give guys like that all my money. I wanted to learn how to do this myself.

Remember the story I told in a previous chapter about Russ von Hoelscher asking me, "Hey, why didn't you just let me write that full page ad for you?" **It was because I wanted to learn to do this myself.** (Russ wasn't the braggart I was talking about earlier, just to clear that up). I was intrigued by this idea that you could put words on paper that would cause people to give you money. It still intrigues me, after all these years. It's fascinating.

Here's another cautionary tale about another freelance copywriter we hired, a very famous guy in our market; I won't call him by name. This was about 16 years ago, and we paid him thousands of dollars. He came and spent a couple of days working with us, staying in our home. Here I am, trying to teach myself how to become a good copywriter—and I'm really putting a lot of effort into it. By this point, my sales letters had collectively generated millions of dollars, so I must have been doing something right! I was really trying to be good, and I was studying everything I could. In fact, I was spending huge sums of money building my library and collecting all types of material that I studied religiously, really putting the time into it.

Well, I had this one letter that I had written, and I was *so* proud of it. I had spent a couple weeks on it by then, so I grabbed it and I showed it to him. He's sitting at our dining room table, and he looks at my letter... well, he doesn't really look at it at all. He just glances at it, flips through a couple of pages, sets it aside, and says, "I can do better." I was enraged, because I'd spent so much of my time and put so much of myself into this letter. For him to flip through a couple of pages and then be a jerk about it just pissed me off. I wanted to throw the guy out of my house, because he was enjoying my hospitality while putting down something I cared deeply about. That's like saying someone's child is ugly. It's just very insulting.

But that anger drove me. It made me want to become even better. That rage grew, and made me even more determined to succeed. **Anger equals determination for me. That event was a big thing for me, actually, because it caused me to want to become the very best writer I could possibly be.** I doubt that's what he intended, but that was the result; and while I'm still angry with him, I thank him for making me a better writer.

My third story involved the same gentleman on another project. Again, we had paid this man huge sums of money, and he actually produced an infomercial for us. We gave up a couple of weeks of our time to go shoot this infomercial, too. The infomercial asked people to raise their hands and send away for the information on this project we were selling, and we ran it in 15 different test cities. We generated upwards of thousands of leads... but then we couldn't convert enough of those leads to sales. I was working the midnight oil to do it, too, putting in a tremendous number of hours developing the sales material that was sent to these people. We were making sales, but not enough to cover the expense. And I'll never forget what happened when we next met with this gentleman—the same man who put my sales letter down on the table and told me he could do better.

I was telling him about all of the struggles I was going through, and all the work that I was doing, and how much effort I was putting into this—and he just kept saying, **"You're giving up on them too soon," meaning that I wasn't doing enough with the leads to convert them.** This went on for well over an hour... and, again, he was kind of a jerk about it. Again, I wanted to kick the crap out of him... although I'm not a violent person. But I just was so enraged!

And you know what? In the end, he was right. He was right about *both* of those things. That sales letter that I had slaved over so hard, only to have him dismiss it, wasn't good enough. **It didn't do an effective enough job in selling.** It didn't make as good a case as it should have. My letters nowadays are a million times better than that one. So he was right: it didn't have enough selling power. And he was right about that second thing, too. I was giving up on those people way too soon.

Nowadays, we relentlessly go after any leads that we generate. In an attempt to upsell, we'll send them many different sales letters that are all little chips off the bigger block. They're easy to write; in fact, in this field there's nothing easier to write than a follow-up letter, because you're just taking bits and pieces out of the bigger block of sales material you already wrote, putting the new beginning and ending on it, and adding a unique a call to action.

As right as this fellow was, what drove me was the anger he inspired. **The angrier I got, the more determined I got; that made me want to spend the time and make the effort to succeed.** And it *was* a substantial effort on my part; I've never claimed to be the sharpest pencil in the box. Chris Lakey picked up on all this a lot faster and easier than me, for example. But my anger caused me to want to pay that price. **So I want you to realize all the benefits of becoming a copywriter, and I want *you* to be willing to pay that price yourself.** I won't try to make you angry, but know that that there's a lot to be said for that approach. When people really make you upset, they make you want to prove them wrong. **And anyway, when people tell you that you can't do something, what's the first thing you want to do? You want to *do* it.**

That goes double for things like being told we can't do something because we're not supposed to, when we *want* to do them. It's just human nature; even if we're told we can't physically do something, that it's not possible, we still want to try. So if someone tells you that you're not going to make the Little League team, you might just decide to do everything you can to make it. **If someone tells you that you can't do anything, the first thing you want to do is prove them wrong.** That anger, that frustration that you feel from being told you're not going to be able to do something, fuels the energy and the passion behind trying to make it so, and trying to prove them wrong. It's a great motivator.

On the other hand, I don't think this guy's method of motivating me was the best possible choice. I think you have to be careful, as a teacher, not to expect too much of the student in the beginning. **You don't want to damage the student's ego with excessive early criticism.** That's certainly not my style!

Let's be realistic. If you're just learning how to write sales copy, you're not going to know everything that someone who's been writing sales copy for 20 or 30 years knows. It's just not possible, and that's fine. You have to keep that in mind as the student, and you also have to keep that in mind if you're teaching someone how to write sales copy. **You can count on us to do that. We may push you, but we're not going to be harsh or rude about it.** If you decide that you want to be a good copywriter, then yes, we've got some strategies and principles that can help you. But we won't expect you to master copywriting after one lesson, or one session, or one chapter, or one audio program, or a few weeks of learning a few basic principles. It just takes longer than that. You have to realize this as well, in your heart of hearts. An amateur copywriter's first sales letter simply isn't going to be nearly as good as their fifth sales letter, or their tenth, or twentieth, or 100th or 1,000th. **They're going to progressively get better, hopefully.**

And don't try to go it alone. They say that when you're learning how to play a musical instrument, it's best to start playing with people right away. Play in a band, or otherwise get some other people together and jam. If you're an electric guitarist, find a bass guitarist, a drummer, and a keyboardist, and just start jamming. The more you play with people, the more you start to get the feel for how to play better; and as you learn, you improve.

With copywriting, you're not going to be a master sales letter writer or copywriter from the first letter... but that still doesn't mean you don't need to get the first one out of the way. **So don't be afraid of not knowing everything.** Don't be afraid to just get out there and start writing sales copy, and don't be afraid to mail your sales letter or put a website up with your sales letter on it, even if it's not as good as it might be if you were an expert. **The only way you get to be an expert is by first being an amateur or a novice.**

Chris Lakey and his wife are currently teaching their oldest daughter how to drive. Chris' wife hates being in the car with their daughter, because it makes her nervous... and they butt heads a lot anyways. Their daughter is 14 now, so the basic mother-daughter problem comes out while she's learning to drive, and it really drives his wife nuts. Chris is a little better, he says, but it's very nerve-wracking to teach someone how to drive. Occasionally his daughter will ask, "Why do you do it this way?" And Chris will reply, "Well, I do it that way because I'm an expert driver. I've been driving for 20 years." She's constantly asking him why he's doing something, and he has to check himself. He might wonder, for example, *Am I doing something wrong? If I'm speeding, I don't want her to think that speeding's okay just because you're an expert driver.*

So he has to be real careful there. But things like turning a corner a little faster than he would want her to—well, he's okay with that, because he has the experience to do it. He wants her to turn really slow because she's learning. There are things she'll do when she's been driving for 20 years that she can't do today because she's just learning. Well, it's the same thing with writing sales copy. **Your sales letters as an amateur copywriter, as a baby copywriter, are going to look different than your sales letters as an experienced professional who's been doing it for a while.**

But you can't let that stop you from doing it, just like Chris can't let the fact that his daughter doesn't really know how to drive that well keep her from driving. The only way she's going to get better at driving is by driving. **The only way you're going to get better at writing sales copy is to write sales copy, so don't be afraid to put yourself out there.** Don't be afraid of "failure," of not getting the results you're looking for. **It's only failure if you refuse to learn, so get out there and keep doing it!** Don't let people tell you that your sales letter's no good. If they tell you that, well, let it go in one ear and out the other. Don't let it keep you from moving forward, and don't let it keep you from pursuing and expanding your ability to write sales copy. Especially don't let it get in the way of your learning more about the whole subject..

And again, that applies whether you're trying to be a freelance writer or whether you're trying to write for yourself or your own company. **If you want to be a good copywriter, you've got to be a bad copywriter first—because at least that means that you're writing copy.** Do what I do: commit to a certain number of words every day and just try to get your thoughts down on paper. Write whatever you're thinking about as it relates to your business and commit to it, even if it's just 100 words, or 500 words, or 1,000 words a day. **Just start writing; by writing something, you'll get better at it.**

And don't ever give up your education as you learn the

strategies and tricks, because there are so many—and it's a never-ending battle to try to stay on top of them. **Let the strategies come, know your marketplace, and just start writing.** You'll get better at it and you'll start to have fun with it, and you'll see how much profit you can make by being a good copywriter. **And look at the end results! When you do get good at what you do, then you could spend a few days or a week writing a sales letter that can generate hundreds of thousands or millions of dollars.**

That is powerful. **If you do it for your clients, they're going to be clients for life.** If you're doing it for yourself, hey, there are a lot of benefits there, too

CHAPTER SIX:

Getting Started as a Copywriter

In this chapter, I'll discuss what it's going to take to get started as a direct response copywriter, outlining both some of the struggles that we've had to go through, and some of the shortcuts that have helped us become experts at it. Not that we're not always improving, because we are; **but these are the tips, tricks, and strategies that got us to the point where we're able to write sales letters that bring in hundreds of thousands, or in some cases even millions of dollars each.** And again, I'm not trying to brag about the money we're making; I only want to brag about just how lucrative this profession can be.

I'll just start with just a couple things. First of all, I believe, just as Russ von Hoelscher told me over two decades ago, that **you can always make more money by writing copy for your own products than you ever can as a freelance copywriter—and that includes projects where other people pay you royalties on the sales you generate for them.** When Russ told me that, he changed the course of my career as a copywriter, so now I'm passing that along to you. If you do choose to go that route, then the best advice that I can give to you is to find a market that turns you on. **Find a market you're absolutely passionate about.** That's good advice for *any* copywriter, actually.

And what is a market? Simply put, it's any group of people who have something in common that causes them to buy certain products and services. The market that we got into was one that really excited me, and still excites me, after all these years! Even now that I know the dirty, dark side of the market that we're in, even after I've gone through some very challenging times, I still love this market! The market we chose, **the market I was passionate about, was the business-opportunity market: specifically, lower-cost business opportunities that you can start for hundreds or thousands of dollars, but definitely for less than $5,000-$10,000.** That's the market we've been in for over two decades. It's a wonderful market to be in, because people are desperately seeking a way to make money—always. There are all kinds of magazines you can advertise in, where other people are selling their own business opportunities and the buyers are looking for the sellers, and there are all kinds of mailing lists that you can mail to, full of people who have inquired about or purchased similar types of moneymaking plans and opportunities.

Choosing this market was the single greatest decision that we ever made. That one decision was responsible for making us many, many millions of dollars; because, again, I was excited about the market. **It turned me on, and I knew a lot about this marketplace already.** You see, for years I personally had been sending away for all kinds of moneymaking plans and programs. My name was on all the mailing lists already; I was getting all the magazines. I was already spending every last dollar I had—and even spending money that I *didn't* have, writing hot checks in some cases. I didn't have a credit card back then, thank goodness, or it would have been maxed-out.

This was in the mid-1980s, and I was hungry for an opportunity. I *knew* that there was a way for me to make a lot of money, even though a lot of my friends and family told me I was destined to always remain a factory or construction worker, basically doing unskilled labor for my entire life. I knew that there was something better out there for me, so I started sending away for all these moneymaking plans and programs; and then the people that I purchased those plans and programs from, as well as the companies where I inquired about their plans and programs and then didn't buy, traded and bought and sold my name. **Pretty soon my name was on all the mailing lists. I'd come home from work and I'd find my mailbox full of interesting stuff.**

Now, I hated my job. At the time, I was working as a welder in a mobile-home factory, coming home hot and tired and dirty every single day. And I'd go to my mailbox, and here would be all these wonderful sales letters that people had written, and postcards and brochures on these various business opportunities. They promised they could give me the dream that I was looking for in exchange for the money they were looking for... and **so I was spending every last available dollar that I had on all of these plans and programs.**

What I didn't know then was that **the writers of the best ads and postcards and brochures, the ones that really interested and excited me, were painting the picture that they wanted me to see; and I was seeing it.** I was a hot prospect, because, again, I hated my job and wanted more out of life. I'd gotten into the habit of re-buying all these different moneymaking plans and programs, looking for that one program that was going to make all the difference in the world, that was going to turn everything around for me—just like we're hoping that this program turns things around for you. Knowing what I know now, I can see that it wasn't the best plans and programs that I spent money on. **I purchased the ones that were sold with the best sales letters.** *Those* were the ones I gladly spent my money on; and in some cases, I probably cheated myself out of some really good moneymaking programs that weren't promoted by somebody who had a passion for what they were selling, or who had no talent for expressing that passion in print.

In other words, I bought those moneymaking plans and programs because the copywriter knew how to sell them. When my wife Eileen and I got into this business, we tried a whole bunch of these programs; and ultimately, we failed on most, and had a lot of really bad experiences. We broke even on others. It was a real up-and-down roller-coaster journey for us. **In the end, we ended up combining a couple of different programs to create our own program that was totally unique, but contained elements of those other two other programs.** We ended up selling this program ourselves—and within the first five years, we generated over $10 million in total revenue.

And you know what? **I wasn't even a good copywriter at the time!** I look back at the copy I wrote back then, and I scratch my head. **The only reason that copy worked was because I was extremely passionate about what I was doing, and I conveyed that in a good enough manner to get other people excited about it also and, therefore, to give us their money in exchange for our program.** After that initial success, we continued to develop more programs that we sold to people on what we call "the back end." The **"front end"** is a marketing term for all the things you do to make that initial sale; the **"back** end" is comprised of all the marketing activities intended to resell to those people. With the help of Russ and other consultants we hired early on, we developed a line of additional products and services that we sold to our buyers on the back end.

We succeeded in our business dreams because I knew the market so well. I knew the people that I was selling to because I was just like them, and I had a passion for all this. **Plus, we told our story in the sales letters, and built relationships with these people.** We made them feel like we knew them, because we really did feel that way ourselves. **There were so many things we had in common with them, and that's still our bond to our customers and prospects to this day.** Even after serving this opportunity market for over 20 years, we still tell our rags-to-riches story, and we talk about things we have in common with people that we've never met and we'll probably never speak to directly, but who continue to do business with us.

There's nothing more important to copywriting success than the market you choose. Find one you're passionate about! Look for a market where people have a history of becoming rabid buyers. That's another term that we use: rabid buyers. These are people who get really hot for a certain type of product or service, and then continue to buy those things like crazy. **There are some markets that are just more profitable for you because the buyers are rabid.** Everybody wants to know, "What do I sell? What do I sell?" Well, if you start with the market first, and think about the people you want to sell to, that goes a long way to coming up with the right products and services. **The market—the people you sell to—is always more important than the products or services you sell.**

About Models

In an earlier chapter, I told you about how I wrote my first little ad. I took a whole weekend to do it, despite the fact that it was a tiny thing, just one-sixth of a magazine page. I looked at all these competitor ads that I knew had been running in the moneymaking magazines forever; I spread them all out on the floor, and I took little elements from each of them. **I didn't plagiarize, but I took the ideas they expressed, looked at the ways they expressed them, and took one bit from here and another from there until I'd pieced together my own, unique ad.** They became my models for what I wanted to achieve.

You *need* models. The ads, sales letters, and websites that other people are successfully using, the ones you see used repeatedly because they work, become the road maps for you to develop your own. If you look at enough of those models from the market you want to serve, you'll see commonalities. **You'll see the same kinds of ideas used again and again.** Those are the major selling points that you need to incorporate into your sales material and develop your products and services around, because if everyone's using them, then they must work.

The good news is, there are plenty of models out there for you to use. What you want to do is look for marketplaces that are extremely rabid, the ones with a lot of competitors. **See, some people don't realize that a lot of competition in a marketplace is a good thing.** They see a market where a whole bunch of people are competing and say, "Oh my God, I can't go into that market." They want to gravitate to a marketplace where there's little or no competition, which is a mistake, because there's no competition there for a reason. The reason is that there's not much money to be had. **No; aim for a busy, competitive market. If there are many competitors in that market, then it proves there's a lot of money being made...** otherwise all those competitors would not exist. Look for lucrative markets, and run your initial ads in the same places where you see the largest percentage of the other people serving your market running *their* ads.

People with no marketing experience often wonder why Burger King would put a restaurant right next to a McDonald's, or why all these retail stores would go up around Wal-Mart. They wonder why these businesses would want competition so close by. In the case of McDonald's, the fact remains that no matter where a McDonald's is situated, they're probably drawing a crowd of hungry people. **So if you have a fast food restaurant close to McDonald's, you're going to get a portion of that business. People are coming to that area looking for a place to eat, so that may mean they'll pick you instead of McDonald's.** That's why you usually see fast food places clustered together: they're putting their restaurants where the hungry people are going to be congregating.

So if you're planning to open a new restaurant, you probably want to find out where other restaurants are in your town, and **you want to put it as close to them as possible.** Some people might think, "Well, all these restaurants are over here on the east side of town, so I don't want to be where they are; therefore, I'm going to put my restaurant on the west side of town." But that's a mistake, because as a result, the new restaurant's not going to have very many customers. **You need to go where you know there's a built-in draw for the type of people you're trying to attract.** This is another type of model for you to learn from. As Willie Sutton is reputed to have said, "I rob banks because that's where the money is." So look at what's already out there, and direct your marketing to where the money is—whether that involves physical location or, as in our case, methods and strategies of writing marketing copy.

In the latter instance, **I think the best thing you can do is start by getting on the mailing lists of the best direct response marketers you can find, and start buying things from them. Get all their follow-up sales material, and watch what they do.** Read their letters, study how they're making their entire sales presentation, and note what a good job they're doing. Learn from that; soak it all up. That's the same way a musician learns how to play songs. They start out by playing other people's music... almost nobody just starts writing their own, and if they do, it sucks anyway. After several years of studying other people's music and mastering certain techniques, they learn how to write their own music... which coincidentally sounds a lot like the music they learned how to play to begin with. It's not especially fast, maybe, but it's a simple and efficient way to learn.

Any time you start thinking, "Oh my God, this is too much to learn," just remember, it's worth the effort! **Learning to write good copy can make you more money than most doctors or lawyers ever dream of making**—and you can do so in a fraction of the time that they took to get all their training. **You can actually earn while you learn, too, as long as you choose a lucrative market you already have an interest in.**

Refining Your Marketing Skills

So, how do you go from just thinking about writing sales

copy to being good at it? **Well, there are any number of books that will teach you technique, business strategies, and all the other things you need to know to sell to your marketplace.** They're fairly common, in fact; you can go to any general bookstore and find marketing books detailing how to reach your target marketplace. Some of these books offer good advice, and some do not.

Again, becoming a good, profitable copywriter starts with your marketplace. **Before you figure out what you want to sell, you need to decide who you're going to sell to; it's as simple as that.** You should get into a marketplace that gets you excited; the more excited you are, the more likely you are to sympathize with your audience, and this will spur you on to write more—and if you write a lot, you can't help but get better as a result. You have to remember that the marketplace comes first, always.

It's best to pick a marketplace that you're very familiar with already, as I did. I was in the marketplace as a consumer long before I was in the marketplace as a business owner. Now, there are a lot of industries that you could do that with. The question is, what industry should you choose? **First of all, you have to pick one with a lot of people in it.** If you're highly interested in something that's very narrow in scope, some very tiny marketplace—maybe some off-the-wall technique for crochet, or writing *Star Trek* fan fiction—then you might want to choose something else. Even if you know a lot about this subject and are really excited about it, you're not going to make much money if you're one of only three people in the U.S. that are interested in it. Unless you're up to the uphill challenge of creating interest among people who aren't already interested, I would recommend that you stay away from that kind of thing.

As I discussed in an earlier chapter, Chris Lakey is interested in golf—though he doesn't get to play much anymore with six kids at home. As someone who enjoys golfing, he can get excited about the idea of new techniques that might shave a few strokes off his game. If he can figure out how to putt or drive better, those things are important to him. And the marketplace is huge: millions of people golf, and most of them are amateur at best. **Even if you ask the pros, they'll tell you they're not done learning.** Everybody who golfs is constantly trying to improve their game, and collectively they spend billions of dollars a year on such things. So if you're an avid golfer, then the golfing marketplace is a good one to get into. Now, you might say, "Yes, I like golfing, and I realize that's a big marketplace. But how does that help me write sales copy?"

It's important to remember that selling is, in many ways, simply the transfer of emotion from you to the person you're selling to. So let's say you're out on the course, waiting for your turn to tee off at the seventh hole. When your turn comes up, you grab your brand new driver—and it's really nice-looking, almost a work of art. You step up to the tee box, you hit the ball—and watch as it sails straight down middle of the fairway, going further than your friends have ever seen you hit before. You're excited, they're all amazed, and then you happen to turn around and say, "You should go get yourself one of these things. This is the best club I've ever had! You saw my game before—you saw how average I was. Well, since I got this club a couple months ago, I can't believe how straight and how far I'm hitting the ball. I got this club over at the Golf Warehouse, and it's on sale right now for only $199. It's regularly $299, but they've got it for $100 off. You should go pick one up while it's still on sale, because it'll do amazing things for your golf game, just like it has for mine."

You're able to sell this product because you're excited about it. If they're in the market for a new driver, or if they're looking to improve their game, they're going to at least pay attention to you—and there's your marketplace. **You've given them the opportunity to purchase a tool that will help them achieve the better golf score they're looking for.** That's all selling really is. For a couple of guys on a golf course, it's one of them telling the other how enthusiastic, how *excited* they are about a product that's helped them improve their game.

Well, if you have the ability to sell that golf club instead of just telling someone where to go get it, all of a sudden you've got the potential for a profitable business! You can write sales copy to convey that enthusiasm in the same manner you did when you were talking to your buddies on the golf course. You can do that in print, on social media like Twitter or Facebook, or even on a YouTube video. The latter might be especially useful for this particular case, since you can show people how hard you hit the ball and how far it goes using this club. You can create an offer and say, "Hey, for the next 10 days this club is available through me for $199 instead of $299."

That's how it's done. **Writing sales copy is just the process of transferring your excitement and enthusiasm to somebody else; that enthusiasm is what gets them to buy.** If you're on a golf course, and someone can see that you're excited about this driver, if they can see the results because you've shown them, then they're more likely to buy. Now, obviously, if you're selling by mail or in some other form of print, you're not showing people something first hand. **But you can include testimonials from people who've improved their golf game, for example.** There are plenty of tools you can use to encourage sales, even if you're not standing right there in front of someone. **You can show them** *proof* **that your product achieves the results that they're looking for.**

The ideal end result is that you've convinced the prospect that this product you're offering will achieve the results that you're promising it will, all due to the enthusiasm you've transferred to them. You've done a good job of convincing the prospective buyer that there's good reason why you're excited to be sharing this information with them, and they should jump on board and make a purchase, whatever the product or service is. I'm using golf as an example, but it can be anything: a business opportunity, a fishing lure, a video game, a book, whatever.

Recently, Chris Lakey spent a weekend near Branson, Missouri with a bunch of guys, and about half of them golf and half of them fish. Chris is a golfer, but he likes to fish, too—**and the fishing marketplace is another that's full of rabid buyers who are looking for any angle they can use to catch more fish.** That means they'll buy all kinds of lures and baits, rods and reels, boats, anything they feel will give them an advantage over the fish that they're trying to catch. That attitude is important to your marketplace, so realizing it—and taking advantage of it—will help you write better copy. Again, marketplace size is also important; the bigger the marketplace the better. **So start with that large, rabid marketplace that you love, and then work to transfer to the people in that marketplace your enthusiasm for the solution that you have to offer.**

A good copywriter can write for any medium, after making a few adjustments here and there. It's all about conveying enthusiasm and transferring that to the prospect. If you start with a marketplace that you're excited about, that gives you a big edge. If, on the other hand, you get into a business that you don't already know a lot about, or it's not a marketplace that you're interested in, then you really have to start from scratch. **You have to learn about your marketplace from the bottom up, and it's a lot harder to gain entry and be successful at it,** because (at the beginning at least) you don't know the emotional triggers that make people respond.

Getting back to the golf industry: Chris golfs, so he knows the frustrations involved. He knows the parts of the game people struggle with, especially driving, chipping, and putting; those are involved in pretty much every aspect of golf. Because Chris knows what people struggle with on the golf course, he could write about it if someone were to come up to him and ask, "Hey, can you help me write a sales letter? I've got this golf product I want to sell." All he would need was some basic information about what the product was designed to do, what part of the game it was designed to help with, and he could write an enthusiastic sales letter that appealed to the golfing marketplace.

Copywriting is always sharpest and most effective when you have a good understanding of the marketplace you're selling to. You don't have to educate yourself before you can start selling. You can do a better job of conveying the benefits the people in the marketplace are going to receive when they do business with you, because you're almost writing to yourself. **That's not to say it can't be done without a prior understanding of the marketplace; it's just that there's a**

bigger learning curve.

The fact, though, is that if you want to succeed as a copywriter, your best bet is to get into an industry that you already know a lot about, an industry that you're already involved in somehow. **In all forms of creative writing (which copywriting certainly is), they teach you to write about what you know. Choose a market that you're familiar with, one that's big and full of rabid buyers, and the writing will be easier, and easier to refine, and far more effective, than if you have to start from scratch with something new.** That's true with any kind of writing you try.

The Element of the Story

The greatest examples of direct response marketing copy tell stories, and for good reason: people remember stories. **Stories contain the necessary emotional elements to effectively convey the benefits that you're trying to sell. Furthermore, they do a powerful job of sliding underneath the buyer's resistance**—their radar, so to speak: the walls that they put up to try not to buy. In many case, people will listen to a story when they won't listen to a sales pitch. **Therefore, you hide your sales pitch in the story, so that it's just one person telling a story to another person.** That's one of the elements that the famous *Wall Street Journal* ad I mentioned earlier used to generate $2 billion in sales.

We're working on a promotion right now, and I'll just tell you how we're putting it together, with the hope that it'll make it easy for you to do something similar. We have a good friend we've been doing business with for about seven years, and he turned us on to this business opportunity that, about four months ago, he wanted us to get involved in; and we did. **We let him use our mailing list, and we provided an endorsement—and that's all we did.** From that point forward, he did everything. He put all the marketing and fulfillment copy together, and he did all the marketing. **Even though we didn't really know much about this opportunity, and we didn't do much, we generated almost $100,000** because of this great sales letter and all the follow-up marketing that he did with our customers.

Well, that got my attention! That woke me up and got me excited. Recently, I spent a while focusing my morning writing sessions on this particular opportunity, because we're getting ready to promote it directly ourselves. Now, I'm not happy unless I write nearly 3,000 words a day, so as of this writing I've written about 30,000 words of copy so far, maybe a little bit more, in nine days—and it's all centered around telling the story of this business opportunity that our friend in Naples, Florida, turned us on to. **I'm also telling people the great story of the $100,000 that came in very quickly, before we really knew anything about the opportunity—and how we're now incorporating the same basic system into this program we're developing for them, so they can have the same advantage.** We're convinced that other people can make as much money as we have, just as easily as we made it—or potentially more, and even faster.

So I'm telling the story, and I'm getting people excited. We're pointing out that our friend from Florida once got a weekly check for $40,500 from the network-marketing company that's part of this business opportunity he's developed and is promoting. I'm saying things like, "Hey, if you think that the $100,000 that we've made so far sounds good, look at our friend who turned us on to this business. In one week, he got a check for $40,500!" **I'm providing all kinds of income examples, playing up all the benefits.**

As I expressed in an earlier chapter, when I write I do what I call brain dumping; I stay very focused on the benefits that I'm trying to convey, the excitement and the enthusiasm, and then just write as fast and furious as I can, putting it all out there. Of course, I'm also trying to do the best job I know how to do; I'm not being lazy and dumping words on the screen just so I can get my word counts. **I'm trying to put my passion into it. I'm trying to share the enthusiasm, I'm expanding on all of the major benefits, and I'm just writing and writing.** Every day, I find exciting, new things to write about, although they all relate back to the main elements we're trying to sell.

This past weekend, I cherry-picked all of the sales copy I've written so far, and put it into the first eight-page sales letter. But that's just the first! We're going to develop all kinds of sales material from these passionate writing sessions, where I just try to tell the story and share the benefits and pour it on and find new ways to compare this opportunity to others, and tell people why I believe that this is the one that can turn things around for our clients. **And I firmly believe that this is something that's going to generate many millions of dollars for our company and our clients, not just because we made $100,000 very quickly, but because of all the elements within the opportunity.** There's a real, raw kind of honesty throughout the copy, because I do firmly believe it.

Selling is the transference of emotions, but it's also the transference of *belief*. The more you believe in something, the more you're going to convey that belief to others. **And of**

course, you have to prove to them that it's real: people are so skeptical nowadays that it's not even funny. Just because you're high as a kite on whatever it is you're selling, that doesn't mean they're going to be. Remember that. **You have to answer all the objections, even before they bring them up. Good copywriting requires salesmanship. Every sales presentation must answer every possible objection.** So spend some time thinking over all the reasons why the prospective buyer might decide not give you their credit card or pull out their checkbook, and try to answer all those objections with something that proves to them that it's in their best interest to give you their money in exchange for what you're selling.

As for the project I'm working on now, I'll probably go for another week before I finally say, "Oh my God, I can't write another word." Finally, the enthusiasm will have worn off completely; I'll have written everything I possibly can, and some things two or three times—always looking for the best possible angle, of course. **Then it's just a matter of editing and reworking it,** which I take care of when things are calm in the evening. I'll have my laptop on my lap, while I'm halfway watching some dumb TV show, and I can just cherry-pick it. Honestly, the rewriting part is relaxing; it's enjoyable. For me, it's the writing part that's intense.

Writing in Phases

To get your work done with maximum efficiency, you need to choose a peak period for your basic writing—the brain-dumping, as I call it. If you're an early morning person, like I am, then get up when it's still dark outside and just start writing, fast and furious. If you're an evening person, do the same at that time of day. **You need to write when your energy is the highest, when your creative powers are at their peak — and you don't worry too much about spellchecking or paragraph breaks or punctuation.** Just try to put as much on the paper as fast as you can, by focusing on the end reader or prospective buyer. It's a kind of performance, really. It's like getting up and speaking in front of a room full of people. You don't want to be boring; you want to say things that get them excited and captivate their imagination and ramp up their enthusiasm. **Tell stories, answer objections, expand on the benefits, show comparisons.**

As I discussed in the previous section, **I think it's best to write in a two-step process, with editing, rewriting, and tweaking coming later.** Of course, when you finish it all, you want it to look like you just sat down and dashed it off... even though you really didn't. Realize that you're never going to create a sales letter in its final form right out of the gate. Understand that it's going to be a mess the first time through; that it's going to require some work to refine and finalize.

That's something that I've always found helpful to consider when looking at other peoples' work. When you receive a sales letter, a brochure or a flyer, or you navigate to a website — you can say this about any kind of sales copy — what you see is the finished product. You don't see all the effort that went into it. Even if you look at it and say, "Wow, that looks like it was written in one sitting," in nearly all cases, it was not. Oh, there may be *some* copywriters who write in one sitting, but they've got to be so rare as to barely exist. That's not the way most people write; certainly, **I don't know anybody who gets it right the first time. Instead, they write in phases — and that's really** the best way to do it. That's the way you should learn to write sales copy, and you'll become a better copywriter for it.

First comes the brain dump: you pick your best time of day to write, and then dump it all out on paper—all your ideas, every thought that comes to mind. **Write down all the benefits, all the promises you can make, all of the descriptions of what you're writing about and what they're going to get when they respond.** You just want to free-flow it. **Let the ideas come.** Again, don't worry about formatting or spell checking, or any of those other things that can cause a bump or hiccup in your writing; **don't spend too much time analyzing or thinking about it.** Sometimes, when I'm writing a first draft, I'll catch myself wondering whether what I'm writing about is workable or not. At that point, maybe I'm writing things that I haven't even thought out very clearly yet; so my mind will start to wonder whether I can do what I'm claiming, or whether what I'm telling my prospect that they can do, or that the system or product can do for them, is accurate. The tendency is to correct as you go.

This isn't the time to analyze! This is the time just to get all the thoughts down. What do you think this could be? What do you think this could do? Here at M.O.R.E., Inc., we deal with a lot of information products, where the product is whatever you want to be. If you're selling a rock, well, there are only so many ways you can describe a rock. You might be able to shape that rock, if you take a chisel to it. You can make it into a square rock or a really smooth round stone. You might be able to describe it this way or that. But generally, a rock is a rock is a rock. There's only so much you can do with it.

But an information product—ah, that can be anything

you want or need it to be. If we're selling a product on, say, how to be a good copywriter, just as an example, we can put whatever information we want into that product. It's an information-based product, after all. If I wanted to write about four key strategies for writing killer sales copy, I could say that this particular product is going to deliver precisely these four important strategies, and work toward making that true. If I wanted to say that I'm going to give you the one secret that will make all your headlines twice as responsive, we can do that. **Ultimately, we're able to make it be whatever we want it to be, because we can focus on and elucidate specific points and aspects of being a good copywriter.**

So you have a little more flexibility in how you write, because you're writing to describe the product. In many cases, we'll write sales copy to sell a product that hasn't even been created yet. Then we'll go in and say, "Well, okay—what did we tell them we were going to tell them?" And then we write to that outline. **We tell them exactly what we told them what we were going to tell them when we wrote the sales letter.** That allows us to be very creative with the words we use to sell the information product.

Admittedly, this can get pretty long. There have been instances when I've mailed Chris Lakey a 70-100 page file after my initial brain dump. Now, we've released a few sales letters that long, but most are much, much shorter. The final sales letter may end up being just 24 pages long. What do we do with all the extra stuff? Some of it gets cut. Some gets modified or narrowed down or honed. **But the only way you get to a 24 page sales letter is to overwrite first. The more you write, the more you have to work with. And it does take a while, because you**

need enough length to pull out the gems.

It would be extremely difficult, comparatively, if you were to try to sit down and write a complete, final 24 page sales letter from scratch with no stops, no breaks, no middle step in the process. Again, there may be copywriters that do that, but I don't know any. Most of them write in phases, like I'm talking about here. **Start by taking the time to get all your thoughts down.** Let it come to you and fill computer screen after computer screen, page after page, with notes and ideas. **Write down any relevant thought. Then go back and you rewrite, and organize your thoughts.** Start writing some headlines; play around with some of the ideas; add more specifics to the offer. **Over several passes of this process, your offer starts to take shape, and your sales letter comes together.** Eventually, you end up with your finished product—but it does take several steps to get there.

Chris Lakey was telling me recently about a golfing friend, an artistic guy who was working on carving a stick he'd found. Chris didn't see him doing the work, but at one point he showed it to Chris and a few of their friends, and it turned out that he had carved into one end of the stick what looked like ram, with curled horns on both sides of its head. It looked really good. It wasn't done yet; but the point is, he didn't just take a stick of wood, make a couple quick cuts and, boom, out comes what looks like a ram's head. He worked on it over a couple of days, doing a little bit at a time, continuing to carve it and shape it and mold it into what he wanted it to be.

That's what you do with a sales letter. You start with a big block of rough copy, rough words, rough ideas. And then, over time, you narrow that down, you carve it, you mold it, and you shape it into what becomes the final sales copy that you use to sell your product. **Writing is done in phases. It's an incremental process, one that takes a lifetime to master... and no one ever really masters it. There are always things to learn.**

Any individual sales letter that you write is like that; it's always a work in progress. I know that Chris and I both have a hard time putting a sales letter down for that reason. We never really feel like it's done; we just have to decide it is. At some point, we feel like it's good enough, even though we never necessarily come to the place where we feel a letter is perfect. **We just have to accept that it's going to be good enough to use.** We have to lay it down and be done with it. I would imagine any other writer probably experiences similar feelings. **Very rarely do you feel like you are completely done with your sales letter. There's always something to tweak, something to change.**

So, you work from this state of raw words; you just put words on a paper, thoughts and ideas all jumbled together; it's very confusing, with a lot of unknowns, a lot of uncertainties as to the finished product and what that will look like. You go from that all the way down to this state where you feel like you can say, "Okay, this is a finished piece." **It's the culmination of a process of narrowing, focusing, honing, and perfecting. At some point you read through it, thinking about your marketplace, and say, "Yes, *this* is an offer that this marketplace wants to respond to.** I know because I'm in this market. I can see them liking this offer. I can see them wanting the benefits that I'm promising here." The copy is ready to go out there and make you money. **That's when you finalize the package, and *then* you're ready to run your ad or mail your**

sales letter.

That's the place where you want to be. And if you've done everything right, if you've matched your marketplace, if you've done your research, if you know your prospects, if you've written a good sales letter that makes them the kind of offer they want to respond to—then the offer can work like crazy. **As Russ von Hoelscher says, all it takes is one good idea, coupled with a killer sales letter, to make a million dollars.** It's happened for us, and it's happened for many other people. Even if we have an offer that *doesn't* make a million dollars, hey, an offer that makes hundreds of thousands of dollars is good! Depending on the kind of lifestyle you're looking for, a sales letter that brings in thousands of dollars can be *very* good for a lot of people. **That's the fun part: bringing in the money after you've written the sales letter.**

In this chapter, I've hopefully given you some good, solid ideas for writing sales copy that you can build on, along with some of the ways that you need to think in order to become a successful copywriter. **If you're serious about taking that next step, then take these concepts in hand and just get out there and start writing.**

I want to wrap up this chapter, and our discussion of copywriting in general, with one final tip. **If you *do* choose to become a freelance copywriter, go into it understanding that every single business has a desire for more sales and profits.** There may be a couple of exceptions you could cite, but they're few and far between. My point is, businesses don't necessarily want to have a brochure or a sales letter written, or whatever the case may be. **What they really want is the results: they're hungry for the sales and the profits.** They can never get enough. Even companies that are doing well financially want to make more money. *Every* company wants more results.

That's why the demand for good copywriting is so high. You're not going to appeal only to those companies that are struggling; in many cases, your best clients will be businesses that are doing good and want to do better, or doing great and want to continue to do great. **They're looking for ways to beat their current controls.** If they already have sales material that's working, they're not satisfied with that; **they want more, more, more!** So drill that idea into your head. **They're all looking for more sales and profits.** That's ambition, and ambition is insatiable. All business owners are ambitious; and with all of the high costs of doing business, they'd better be focused on making more sales and profits or they're going to lose their edge in the marketplace. If that happens, they might not be around much longer.

Good sales copy that brings in the cash is music to their ears. They want and need more sales and profits. **They're looking for bigger results, so they're looking for talented people who can provide those results.** That is the sole purpose of a freelance copywriter, especially in direct response marketing, where the results can be tracked. **That's the most important thing; now all you have to do is get your foot in the door.** All you have to do is wake these people up, get them to pay attention to you, and convince them to let you do that initial job that will lead to them becoming lifelong clients. It's that simple. **It's not *easy*, obviously, but it's just that simple. Remember that. Anytime you're frustrated, just go back to the basics.** You get your foot in the door with that initial job, handle it professionally and in a way that makes the customer happy, and from that point forward, you build a relationship with them so they remain your client for years.

So how do you get your foot in the door? You have to mail them a sales letter. Start with the envelope; we get ours from a company called Uline. Get a 9-by-12 envelope with a full window. On one side, it's nothing but clear cellophane; you can put the business owner's address on the other. What you send to them is a copy of the ad that they're currently running. If it's a sales letter or postcard, you just take the whole thing and glue it onto a piece of paper; and right above that write, "I can make you more money with this ad." Then you maybe point to it, or highlight it with a pen or something like that. **Enclosed with that is your sales letter that sells them on your freelance copywriting services, and shows them how you can help them make more money.**

You see, business owners are very, very busy, and they're constantly being bombarded with all kinds of stuff from people who want their business. It takes more to get through to them, and this is the way for you to do it. **This is a direct-mail package that they just can't resist. They'll have to open it up. It's *their* ad.** They spent money on that ad. This is their baby. It's their pride and joy. As they're separating their mail over the trash can (as most people do), they're going to spot your envelope with their ad sticking out, and they'll put it aside so they can look at it later. When they have more time, they'll give it the attention it deserves.

At that point they'll read your sales letter, and if you make them a really good pitch, they'll probably hire you. It depends on the offer you make, and how persuasive you are. Now, it's a simple idea, but there's no better way to go if you're going to do freelance. It does cost more money to do it that way, of course; but, dollar for dollar, you're never going to get better results.

So take the time to use that simple idea. **If you do become a client of our Get Paid to Write coaching program, we'll give you a sales letter that Chris and I developed that sells an initial consultation service, and we'll even help you by partnering up with you to provide some of those initial services.** So it'll be like using training wheels on a bike. I'll tell you a little bit more about that as I wrap up this book, but I wanted to go ahead and plant that seed right here and now. **We have a way for you to become a freelance copywriter and start getting paid immediately, by letting us work with you until you have enough confidence that you'll want to cut us out completely and go forward on your own.**

That is an open invitation to all members of our Get Paid to Write coaching program! Remember, this is something that can make you financially set for life. **There's a learning curve involved; you can go through that learning curve yourself, or we can help you get through it with our coaching program.** We'd like to do that. It's not just about the money, although we do make money when we sell our coaching memberships. But we are also very, very passionate about this— and there's nothing we'd like more than to help you learn this wonderful way of making money.

CHAPTER SEVEN:

The Ghostwriting Option

In this chapter, I'm going to talk about one aspect of writing that can make you money right away, and can ultimately earn you a six-figure annual income. The subject is ghostwriting. Now, you've probably heard of ghostwriters. For the most part, the celebrities who "write books" aren't really writing those books themselves. **They use a ghostwriter for the actual work;** sometimes they list the name of the ghostwriter on the credits, but oftentimes they don't. The point is, you can rest assured that every year, thousands of the books (and many other things) that are published are written by people other than the ones claimed as the author.

The Literary Urge

People use ghostwriters because, quite frankly, writing is hard work. Many of the people who want to get their ideas out there in the public venue aren't particularly good writers, and they may not have time to become good writers. In either case, it's easier for them to let somebody else do it. **Here at M.O.R.E., Inc., we've used a couple of ghostwriters throughout the years.** I'll tell you a couple stories about the ghostwriters we've used in moment, and how those ghostwriters have made us a tremendous amount of money while also helping themselves make good money.

But before I do, let's take a quick look at the world of business. Most businesspeople know that it's advantageous to differentiate themselves from all the other businesses in their particular marketplace; that's a basic foundation of any business. **There's a real advantage for them to become an expert, someone with a strong voice—and one way to do that is to publish a book related to the type of products and services that the business provides.** That really makes them stand out. And the fact is, being an author is something that a lot of people want in the worst sort of way. You've heard the cliché, where people say, "Well, I could write a book about that," or, "I've got a book in me." It's a popular cliché; and like all clichés, it represents a real truth.

People want to be famous in their market. It's good for business, and it's good for their egos—and most business owners and entrepreneurs have strong egos. **A book can help catapult them to the top even faster.** Look at our current President: at the time of this writing, Barack Obama has written two books. I haven't read them, but I've listened to the abridged audio of both books, and it's clear that those books helped him rise above all his contenders. That's what a good book can do.

A book can build bonds with people. You become an expert when you become an author; you have status now. People want to do business with other people who are the experts, the authorities, the people they can have total confidence in; and when they see that you've written a book, it elevates you. **Or at least, it can *potentially* elevate you, depending on how you market that book and what you do with it.**

There's a huge need for ghostwriting out there, because every entrepreneur and every politician has (by necessity) a giant ego. The direct mail letter that we've put together for you, if you choose to become a client of our Get Paid to Write coaching program, is a letter that you can send out to all of the local businesspeople and politicians in your area in which you offer to write a book for them. **That book can be based on something as simple as you interviewing them and recording that conversation. It doesn't even have to be face-to-face; it can be right over the telephone.** Record that conversation, have it transcribed, rewrite it, and let them be involved in the final editing stages. **It doesn't have to be that difficult if you've got the writing skills, or if you want to develop the writing skills.** It's something that will provide real value to them that you can charge good money for, and that's why there are plenty of ghostwriters out there. Just Google "ghostwriters," and you'll see there's a whole bunch of people offering such services.

Again, that should never dissuade you. Instead, it should *encourage* you; it's a positive thing! It shows that there's a real demand out there for ghostwriting services, and just because there are some heavy hitters in the business who are knocking down huge dollar amounts doesn't mean that you can't find your niche and provide a good living for yourself by doing what you love. **And understand that writing is some of the hardest work in the world, which is why it's worth the premium rate that you'll charge.**

Realize too, as I've mentioned earlier in this book, that **your clients just want the results; really, that's how it works in any business.** If you're a freelance copywriter, they just want sales material that's going to deliver results. If you're the ghostwriter, they just want to see a book in their hands that's got their name on it as the author. **They want to see their ideas**

expressed in a written format. It's good for their ego, and it's good for their business or their political career; or if they just want to pass that book around to their family and it becomes a family heirloom, it could be something that will live on for many generations after they're gone, and could be something of real value down the road for somebody else. Those are the benefits of publishing.

Lessons from Our Ghostwriting Experiences

The first ghostwriter we hired, Steve Lockman, passed away a few years ago. Steve was a good man. We only actually met him once when he came to Kansas, because Steve lived clear up in the northern part of Minnesota, in a small town just six miles south of the Canadian border. He wrote dozens of booklets and reports for us, along with some newsletters. Initially, we hired him when we were running our original sales promotion, for a program called "Dialing for Dollars." This was a way for our distributors to make money by selling our booklets, using a telephone answering machine to replace a live salesperson. **We had almost 30 booklets. Steve wrote all of them, except for maybe two or three. We sold them to our distributors at wholesale... and just at the wholesale level we sold millions of dollars of the books that Steve produced.**

We couldn't keep him busy enough! The four or five years that promotion ran, Steve did a lot of work for us, and later we continued to use him for different things. **Basically, we'd tell Steve the titles of the booklets that we wanted him to write, and sometimes we would give him reference books that were similar to it.** Otherwise he would do his own research, and create the booklet from there. **This process helped us make a**

lot of money—and we didn't have to actually do the work, which was the real benefit to us. Steve kept pounding out new titles, and we kept paying him good money. **Steve was handicapped, so he was in a wheelchair, and he had serious health problems—and yet he was able to get paid writing.**

We met our second ghostwriter about five years ago, when we needed someone to convert some of our printed transcripts into a more readable format—because when information is taken straight from audio to transcript without some massaging, there's often something lost in the translation. **For example, this book started as an audio program before going to our ghostwriter. His name is Floyd Largent, and he lives in San Antonio, Texas.** In the five years he's been with us, Floyd has ghostwritten literally thousands of pages! **What he does is take our transcripts—just like the audio transcripts we're doing for this particular program—and cleans them up, edits them, and does a little rewriting here and there.**

You see, just because you can understand an audio recording doesn't mean that the written transcript isn't loaded with problems... because it inevitably is. You'd be surprised how much the two venues, audio and printed, can differ. **There are many, many things that a good writer can do to convert a transcript to a more readable format.**

When we started looking for a ghostwriter a bit over five years ago, we had a need for a tremendous amount of work of this type. Our goal was to produce a series of books that were based on the best of the best of all of our marketing tips, tricks, and strategies, so we went onto Elance.com, a site where freelancers of all kinds can bid for work. **You just post the kind of work you want done, and collect the bids.** We did that, and ended up with 34. In our posting, we told the bidders that we were an information marketing company with a need for a ghostwriter to do thousands of pages for us over the years; we made it clear that this was a long-term request on our part. **We were looking for a good ghostwriter that we could develop a profitable relationship with over the long term... the same way we develop relationships with our clients and customers.**

Thirty-four people replied, and many of them actually said that they would even do some of the work for free—or at least give us some free samples of their work. Well, because we couldn't possibly figure out how we were going to work with 34 people, we reduced the field down to the three that we thought were the best of those who responded. We gave them each a portion of a job to do... and two of them absolutely sucked. Pardon my language, but they were terrible.

Now, these were two of the three that we really thought were the very best, based on the information that they provided and certain things that they said about themselves in their profiles and resumes. But that third one, Floyd Largent—he just shone brightly over all the others. Since that time, he really *has* done thousands of pages for us... and until Floyd decides to stop or something unforeseen happens, he's going to continue being our ghostwriter. **We keep him busy month after month, and he's got plenty of work coming from other people, too.** He's built a thriving business for himself and, of course, we've told some of our friends about him. They're also using him, and I'm sure they've told some of *their* friends.

Look, when you're good, after a while word of mouth just kicks in. So here Floyd is, living in San Antonio, Texas—which is a beautiful city, by the way. If you've never been there, you definitely should add it to your bucket list, and at least go down there once. Floyd has built himself a thriving business there. **Basically, we just give him the printed transcript of our audio programs, just like we're going to give him the transcript of *this* audio program, and he makes it readable, using his talent as a writer to deliver a printed product we can truly be proud of—and that we can profit from.**

There's a huge need for work of this nature. If you've got the writing skills or the desire to do this, it's something you could be providing to others. They've got the knowledge on the subject matter; you can either interview them or ask them to provide you transcripts on whatever they want to talk about, and then you simply reformat it, edit it, and rewrite it as necessary so it contains all their best ideas. **The goal is to make it more readable, something that they can be proud of. If you can accomplish that and consistently do good work for them, they will keep you forever.** They'll never even think about using another ghostwriter, and they'll brag about you to all of their friends, as we have. Word of mouth can quickly spread.

Now, I told you that 34 people responded to the Elance ad that we posted, and we chose the top three. Those other two were no good at all, but did they stay in touch with us? No, they didn't! Not even one email. Did any of the other people stay on top of us? Nope. We posted an ad on Elance telling people that our intentions were to do thousands of pages worth of work, which has proved true. **We chose the best three, but none of the other 31 people stayed after us at all; they didn't follow up.**

Look, you can go out there and buy books on learning the secrets and intricacies of ghostwriting... **but some of this is just common sense.**

I've seen it so many times, in so many places—not just in this example here. People assume that just because somebody doesn't do something for them once, or because something doesn't work out once, that the other person just wasn't interested. In some cases, people are assuming that erroneously. **The client is still interested; they just need a little more persuading, a constant pressure that you have to apply to remind them that you're out there wanting to do the work.**

In this case, Floyd was the winner, and we're lucky to have Floyd; we're very grateful to him. **Our relationship was set into stone with Floyd within just a few months, too.** From that point forward, we wouldn't have considered another ghostwriter. But the truth is, *prior* to that point, somebody else could have gotten in there and possibly have gotten our business. Again, we chose the best three based on the resumes they provided and the information they gave us, but there's no reason for me to believe that some of the others weren't just as talented as Floyd. **What they lacked was the ability to follow up.**

It just makes common sense to keep after the client. Every salesperson knows instinctively that that's how you sell something: **by constantly staying in touch with people, never releasing that pressure, always staying after them...** and yet so many people who are new to business just don't understand this. They think that when somebody says no once, or doesn't do what they intended or wanted done, then that means they're not interested. That's not always the case. **So a word to the wise: be persistent. Be relentless in your follow-up. This is applicable to all aspects of any business.**

When someone responds to a small ad that you might run, telling people that you can provide these copywriting or ghostwriting services for them, then they're showing you that they're very serious. **Just because they don't take advantage the one time, or because they don't respond to the third or fourth follow-up, doesn't mean you can't be creative and use your writing skills to stay in touch with them and communicate with them very effectively.** Because again, once somebody finds a good ghostwriter, they can continue to do business with that person for years. The big hurdle at the beginning is landing their business; once you prove to them that you can do the work professionally and productively, they're hooked. **All you need is a handful of clients who are willing to continue to do business with you month after month, year after year, and you're set.**

You can work from the comfort and privacy of your own home, you can live anywhere in the country you want to live, and you can have a thriving business doing what you do best, which is writing. There's a huge need out there, and if the only thing you get from this book is that firm understanding of just how powerful the demand is for people who can write well, then you've more than gotten your money's worth. All that those potential clients want is the result, the book in their hand. **If you can deliver that effectively and economically, and get your foot in the door, then you can take that relationship to the bank for years.** There's no reason why someone's going to stop with one book, you see, because it's addictive. I know that because we've got about 20 books out there right now for sale on Amazon.com that were all ghostwritten by Floyd.

You know, I find it amusing that I'm talking about ghostwriting on the audio program that's the basis of the book in your hands, and our ghostwriter, Floyd, will be reading these very words in just a short time. After I've done recording these CDs, he'll be perusing the raw transcripts, cleaning them up and editing as he goes. **That makes it sound easy, but you have to realize that ghostwriters are wordsmiths; working with words, and making things readable, is their stock in trade.** They're skilled craftsmen, in their way. That's critical. **If you want to be a ghostwriter professionally, you need to be good at writing;** that's when the business of ghostwriting can be lucrative for you. No one wants to hire a bad writer to do their writing for them! **But remember: this is something that you *can* learn, and if you're persistent, it can pay off handsomely.**

The Competitive Edge

In this section, I'd like to re-emphasize just how strong the demand is for good ghostwriters. Every time we've run ads looking for writers, the response has been phenomenal—even though the writers know that the work is for hire, and they're not getting any official credit for what they produce. **We've always received more responses than we anticipated, which I think is illustrative of the demand.** There are just so many people out there looking that the number of writers has grown large in response; this is a corollary of my observation, in an earlier chapter, **that you want to look for a market with a lot of competitors, since that proves that the market itself is large and profitable.** Of course, that also means there are a lot of bad competitors out there, which makes it a lot easier for you to compete. Just prove you're better than they are!

When we were looking for a new ghostwriter five years ago, Floyd's response and those of the other two people we tried just stood out. Part of that was because of their ability as writers;

even in their brief proposals, something about their responses captured our attention and made us decide to give them a try. In our opinion, just three out of the 34—less than 10%—were worth more than a cursory glance; the others were so dull that we had no interest in even trying them out. **That's because they didn't do a good job of selling themselves; and if they couldn't sell themselves, how were they going to help us sell our products and services?**

So as you think about being a writer—specifically a ghostwriter in this example, but this applies across the board— the first thing you have to remember is you're competing with a bunch of other people who also consider themselves good writers; otherwise, they wouldn't be trying to hire themselves out. **First and foremost, you must sell yourself.** In this case, your talent and ability to write is the only product you have to sell; so you have to approach things a little differently than you would if you were, say, a local retail store selling widgets. **Your writing is not merely your product; it's your advertising as well.** Everything you write now, and everything you've written in the past, is a demonstration of your ability and an argument as to why your prospect should hire you. You can say, "Look at what I did for so-and-so. Here's my portfolio," but the way that you make the pitch also matters, because your writing is how you sell yourself. Never forget that. **Your writing is what makes you appealing, so in addition to being a good ghostwriter, you also need to be a good copywriter as well in order to sell yourself and your service.** You ability to write good sales copy will go a long way towards you being able to attract clients, at least in the beginning.

Of course, once you're established, you'll attract work by

word of mouth. This is what has happened for Floyd; he used to hustle to get work on Elance and elsewhere, but now he has all he can handle, and people approach *him* for work. He rarely has time to take a deep breath these days! But he's loving it, because he has a number of long-term clients, including us, and some of those people we referred to him. He has created and cultivated relationships that are profitable to both him and his clients. **If you become a good, successful ghostwriter, you can get an unlimited number of referrals and pick and choose your work, because people talk about the positive experience they've had.**

If someone says, "Yeah, I'm thinking about writing a book, and I really don't have the time to write it myself, so I need a ghostwriter," someone else might say, "Hey! I know who you should hire. Look at my book. I don't really like to tell people this, but I used a ghostwriter to write it. His name is Bob Smith, and he did a great job, and here's why. I think that he would do an excellent job for you, too." **They become a salesperson for you, doing that work on your behalf.** Because it is a small world at the top of any field, and people love to talk.

After people read a couple of the early books that Floyd did for us, they complimented me on those books. And of course I told them, "I didn't write this myself," and I gave them the name of my ghostwriter. If the people who buy my books ever happen to ask me if they were ghostwritten, I'd happily tell them yes... but they won't. People will just naturally assume that I'm the writer, and all the ideas are mine. That's often the case, but a lot of them are Chris Lakey's, because **many of the books that Floyd has done are transcripts of marketing audio that Chris and I did together.** So *his* best ideas are in there, too. I'm stealing all of Chris's best ideas and putting my name on them!

The point is, once you're established and you've proven yourself to people, word will get around, especially if you become a writer for celebrities. Celebrities who "write books" usually use ghostwriters. If you're interested in politics, there are groups of people who all relate together in political circles. If you're into sports, you can become a really successful sports ghostwriter, because many of those guys know each other. Let's say you've written a bestselling sports book for whoever happens to be the latest and greatest baseball or football or basketball player. Or maybe a famous referee retires, and he's got lots of stories, and you become *his* ghostwriter. Well, word gets around... and all of a sudden you become the go-to person for sports ghostwriting. **Basically, you can make a name for yourself and get all kinds of free publicity just by doing good work for people.**

As I noted earlier, we've used a couple of ghostwriters in our time—and back in his early days with the company, Chris Lakey did some ghostwriting as well. This was about 17 years ago, maybe a bit longer. So let's say that's three ghostwriters, though Chris asks me not to reveal the names of the books he wrote, to protect the innocent! Seriously: one particular manual that he wrote for us, about making money with a computer bulletin board, sold a couple million dollars worth—just that one project. As I recall, he wasn't even 20 years old when he did it. **I think that this example illustrates the tremendous value here: that one manual generated over *two million dollars*.**

You may not (and probably won't) get that kind of response from the very beginning of your ghostwriting career; there's always a learning curve in any subject. And let me re-emphasize the value of Elance and similar services, on both sides of the fence. **If you're serious about being a ghostwriter, Elance can be a good place for you to get started—especially if you're willing to do some cheap work while you're building a name for yourself and deciding what kind of a niche you want to be in.** Unfortunately, there are a lot of people there fighting for jobs, and that means that the price goes down somewhat; that's good from the buyer's perspective, since you can go to Elance and hire a writer pretty cheaply, simply because there's a lot of them on there looking for work.

I would recommend that, beyond Elance, you find other ways to build a client base, and find some people that will pay you more money—because you may not make as much on Elance as you might working elsewhere. **The prices can go higher when you start working by word-of-mouth,** and someone comes to you and says, "Hey, I heard you're the best writer around for this project." At that point, you can say, "Yes, I am... and that doesn't come cheap."

Elance is more of a place to get started, though you can also look on Elance for some subcontractors. Let's say you build this big ghostwriting conglomerate; you're known as the top ghostwriter in this field, and everybody wants you. Well, you can only write so many words yourself... unfortunately, writing is one of those things that's time-based, so if you're not writing, you're not getting paid. But you could use Elance to find a group of good, trusted ghostwriters who have proven themselves. After all, you're getting paid for the quality of your work; you don't want other people representing you poorly. But you *could* build a team. **Let's say you found a team of three very good ghostwriters on Elance who could help you do**

more work than you could do alone. If you found a team who had your accepted level of quality and standards and whom you could work and communicate well with, **you could develop a business in which you can collectively do more and get paid more than you could on your own.**

Ghosting for Fame and Fortune... Well, Maybe Just Fortune

The main thing is just getting your name out there. **If you want to be in the ghostwriting business, it's important to start building that client base and get those referrals.** If you were to do a Google search on "ghostwriting," you'd find all kinds of resources and information on the topic—some of it good, I'm sure, and some of it bad. But there's a lot of stuff out there. **If you're a ghostwriter for hire, you should build a website where you list your references and provide your contact information, and put yourself out there for people to hire.** Do things to build publicity for yourself and make yourself known, because typically, ghostwriters are unheralded. They're private people; no one knows who they are. If you write a book for a celebrity, that celebrity is the one who gets their name in the papers. They're the one on all the talk shows, doing all the interviews on Letterman. They're the one out there in public.

You get paid, literally, to be the ghost. You write the words, but you don't get any general fame or recognition for it. Still, to the people who hire ghostwriters, you can be super-famous! You can be somebody that they know and have in their Rolodexes, or on speed dial on their cell phones. **When they need a book written, hey, they know who to call!** You're the best in the business from the ghostwriting perspective... so they come to you. Even better, they share that information with their friends and anybody who says, "I'm thinking about having a book written." You'll be the one they call, because they know that you're the best.

So within your marketplace, among the people who need your service, you can be famous... you just don't get the celebrity that comes from being the face on the book. **It's sort of an anonymous fame, if you will; you're famous in your own circle, among the people who need what you do.** That's what you get to look forward to as a ghostwriter.

The field can pay very well, and in a bit I'll give you some examples of how much money you can make in the ghostwriting business. **But just realize that there's a lot of need out there for good writing,** because the idea of publishing a book is not going to go away anytime soon, even though we're in the digital age now—even though we have eBooks and things like the Amazon Kindle, and all these other book readers people use these days to read on their mobile devices, not to mention audio books. **The written word is not going away;** there's always going to be a need for skilled writers who don't mind being ghosts, who are fine with putting their work out there for the public without getting name recognition... as long as they get paid. **And in some cases, you can get paid very good money just for being okay with being anonymous.**

Again, it's the worth to the client that can drive ghostwriting prices sky high. A skilled writer is very, very valuable to business people, politicians, and anybody else who wants to become a local celebrity, or get their word out, or just create something that will outlive them—where they share ideas that will be around for generations to come. **The demand is incredibly high... and most people have no idea of just how**

easy it is to have a book, or a report, or any other kind of information product ghostwritten for them.

That's one of the things that the sales letter we've created for the folks involved in our Get Paid to Write coaching program communicates very clearly to the prospect. **It tells them just how simple and easy it can be for them to become an author;** and I think that people will be shocked when they get that letter and learn just how easy it is. Really, it can be as simple as you, the ghostwriter, interviewing them over the course of a few sessions, asking them a bunch of different questions and pretending you're Larry King. **You're bringing out the best ideas that they have inside them, converting those to transcripts, and then using your talents as a writer to polish those transcripts into something readable.**

Once people find out just how straightforward it is, they'll not only hire you the first time, they'll be hooked from that point forward. **They'll get a lot of attention, you see, and that's really what they want.** And I say that while laughing at myself, because I too enjoy having all those books with my name on them!

The One-Eyed Man's Advantage

Earlier, I mentioned a quote from the 16th century that goes like this: "In the land of the blind, the one-eyed man is king." This brings us back to the fact that there are so many people out there who either suck as writers or aren't willing to follow up on their proposals. Remember, of the three top writers we chose out of the 34 people who responded to our Elance ad, two of them were just worthless! The writing was terrible; Floyd's stood out head and shoulders above theirs. But beyond that, they didn't even follow through. **They didn't ask us why we didn't hire them, or what we liked or didn't like; they didn't stay in touch with us or try to do anything to remedy the situation at all.** Had they done that, we may have decided to work with them.

As with any small business category, **most of the people out there trying to make a living as ghostwriters are terrible marketers.** They're just no good at all. **So I would encourage you to be persistent, because persistence really does pay off in business.** Prospects like being courted—and you've *got* to court the prospect. **You've got to stay on top of them, because in many cases, you're not the only provider under consideration.** Plus, they're busy with a million other things, and they only have so much disposable income, which they might choose to spend somewhere else. **You have to be relentless in your follow-up;** you have to do everything you can to stay in touch with them and try to build relationships, using your writing skills to sell yourself.

Here's the saddest part about our Elance experience: **evidently, each of those people who responded felt that they had some skills as a writer... but they didn't really use those skills well.** They could have been sending us regular emails, they could have been finding creative ways to communicate who they were, what they were about, why we were making a mistake by not hiring them, and in general all they could do for us in trying to build that relationship, trying to establish themselves in our minds— and yet they weren't doing *any* of that.

A Few Profitable Pointers

The sales letter that we give you if you join our program does a good job of selling; and one of the key aspects it uses in doing so is the concept of celebrity.

As we've pointed out, most people are unaware that most of the books "written" by the celebrities and hyped on the talk shows are *really* written almost entirely by ghostwriters, based on some of the ideas that we're sharing here. **There's an interview process, and ultimately the celebrity's key ideas are brought forth and polished to produce the book.** It's not their writing skill that does it: it's the ghostwriter's. **So, we play up that celebrity angle.** A lot of people envy celebrities, because they want the same prestige, the same attention, the same money, and the kudos that a celebrity gets.

We tell them that what they need is their own book. **If they just had their own book, they could become a local celebrity in their marketplace;** they can get the attention they want, rising head and shoulders above their competition—they can stand out and be noticed. **In other words, they can have all the joys that come with being an author, without doing the actual writing.** That angle has a lot of appeal to it. It's something that people really, really want, and again, it drives an incredible demand for ghostwriting services. **And then, of course, we make it very easy for people to raise their hands and make that initial contact with you.**

Incidentally, I would suggest that when you're working with a new client, always get some of the money up front. It's very common to ask for half of the money in advance and the rest on completion, so that in case you *do* get stiffed, at least you got some of your pay. This is especially important if you're working with wild and crazy entrepreneurs who are always running into cash flow problems. **And don't be afraid to ask for referrals.** Just because the client won't give you referrals on their own doesn't mean that they won't give them if you ask for them. So be relentless about that. It's a small world at the top, and high-performance people always know other high-performance people. **Usually, they'll be glad to help you if you'll ask for it; and again, use your writing talents and skills and abilities to communicate all these things.**

Another pointer: **spy on your competition.** It's beneficial to do so, and while I know that this is going to sound a little bit crazy, it can be fun and sneaky in an almost childish way. When I was kid, we used to have a lot of fun making prank phone calls. It was a more innocent world back then; they didn't have Caller ID, thank God! We had a blast—and for the most part we didn't upset anybody too bad. This is basically the same kind of thing I would like for you to consider when it comes to spying on your competitors. Pretend that you're a prospect. **Go out to half a dozen or so of your competitors, and pretend you're looking for a good writer.** This will prove to you just how bad these people are at following up the way they should, even those who have good websites and an established clientele. They're not doing a good job of marketing at all.

This should boost your confidence, and you need that confidence in order to get started. **Most of those people just won't follow up with you at all; and if they do, their efforts will be weak.** Of course, you'll also find a few people who will, and this will break your heart just a little; they'll try to build a relationship with you, because they're honestly interested in trying to help. The truth is, you *are* being a little dishonest to those people—because you're pretending to be something you're not, never really intending to use their services. **But don't feel too bad: it's all done with the intention of coming**

to understand the market at that direct experience level, and
it really will boost your confidence to learn how bad the
competition is. You don't have to do it for long, but you should
do it. Spy on your competition; find out just how many bad most
people are, and find out what those few good people are doing in
order to build their ghostwriting businesses.

About Those Income Examples

Earlier, I mentioned some income examples that can
illustrate just how profitable the ghostwriting field can be. Most
of what I'm about to share with you I got from the Internet just
by doing a little research, on Wikipedia and elsewhere, about the
going rates these days. **We know what we pay our ghostwriter,
but what else is out there?**

**One of the things it's important to realize is that
ghostwriters are usually paid by the page,** so traditionally,
you get a flat fee based on how many pages the work ends up
being. **And yet usually, they'll spend some time researching
before the project gets started;** so if you're going to ghostwrite
a book on a certain subject, you might spend months or even up
to a year on research, really getting into the project before you
write a single word. That's surprising to a lot of people, but it's
common. Some of these major celebrity or political books,
especially, require a lot of research—**so it's necessary to make
sure that you get an advance on the work, just in case
something happens.** You might get a big advance to write a
book, even though that book might not come out. Or, it might
not be finished and published for another year or 18 months.

**Wikipedia claims that having an article ghostwritten
can cost $4 per word and more, depending on its complexity.**

We're talking about real technical writing, of course. **One literary agent they quote, Madeline Morel, states that an average ghostwriter advance for major publishers is between $30,000 and $100,000 per book. Imagine that!** That's a wonderful example of the profit potential here, and it can help you decide where you want to go with your ghostwriting. It's not going to happen overnight, but if you can become successful and work your way up to the major publishers, you really could get as much as $100,000 for one book.

The *New York Times* stated that the ghostwriter for Hilary Clinton's memoirs received a fee of about half a million dollars, which they said was near the top of what ghostwriters ever could make. That's something to keep in mind, even if you might think, "Well, it's not anything I could ever do." **But the ghostwriter who got that huge fee started out just like you!** At some point, that person was an inexperienced newbie who realized that they had the skills to be a good writer, and wanted to be a ghostwriter. They got into the business and worked hard, and eventually worked their way up to the point where somebody within Hillary Clinton's circle said, "Hey, we need to have this person as our ghostwriter for this project."

That's a political example, and a lot of political figures have had books ghostwritten. That can happen with all kinds of other people, too. **Celebrities often have books ghostwritten.** People in Hollywood want to tell their story; they feel that people like them and watch them on TV or in the movies, so maybe they should make money with a book. So they hire a ghostwriter; and there's no reason why that ghostwriter can't be you, if you're interested in this kind of thing. **According to Ghostwriting, Inc., a professional ghostwriting service,**

ghostwriting fees average from $12,000 to $28,000 per book.
Not bad. Usually, that's a negotiated price; and then the client
gets to keep all the other advances, post-publishing royalties,
and the profits, if any. You're the ghostwriter, and that's it.
**That's the end of the relationship: a flat fee, and they're
done with you.**

There's a more recent trend of outsourcing ghostwriting
jobs, too. Whereas there used to be a lot more demand for
ghostwriting in the U.S., some companies and individuals have
started looking to other countries for ghostwriting—specifically
India and the Philippines—because sometimes they can save as
much as 80%. **The quality is usually lower, but so is the price.**
They say that in some cases, you can get a complete book for as
little as $3,000 to $5,000—considerably less than in the U.S. **But
if you could get paid S5,000 for a 200-page book, that's $18 a
page; not bad work.** And you do have fun, and get to live the
lifestyle you've dreamed about. You still get to be considered a
writer. You get the glamorous lifestyle, if you will, even though
you don't get all the credit. So $5,000 isn't bad for a book.

People are paying that to outsource to other countries, so if
you could offer that price here, you could get a lot of work. You
might say, "I'll do that same work for the same price. I'll do a
better job, and I'll be right here locally." **They can save the
money and you can still get the business.** You should
definitely consider that as you're thinking about what price you
want to charge for your services.

Categories of Ghostwriting

You've got plenty of choices when it comes to the kind of
ghostwriting you'd prefer to specialize in. **Nonfiction is**

probably the biggest category: celebrities, politicians, and other high-profile people are always wanting books written for them. It's said that two of President John Kennedy's books were almost entirely written by ghostwriters; and President Ronald Reagan had a ghostwriter help with his autobiography. **In other non-fiction areas, business people like us are often in need of ghostwriters to turn our ideas into books, or to take material in one category, like audio, and convert it into print.**

You can ghostwrite religious books and texts, or even medical books. I would assume you'd need to be very detail-oriented in that field, but you could become a medical ghostwriter, if that's something that interests you, and publish a lot of scientific and pharmaceutical books and documents. To me, that would be very boring — but it may be an interesting subject to you, one that you could profit from. The same is true of academic writing. **Again, it's kind of brainy, but if that's your sort of thing, you can certainly make money in the realm of academic ghostwriting.**

Websites and blogs are also an option; everybody has a blog these days, including many businesses. **Some ghostwriters specialize in blogs, and the same is true of websites, especially the content-driven type** — which is most of them. They all need a lot of words on a regular basis, which is why so many people are turning to ghostwriters to fill that need for digital words.

And then there's music. This is something I don't know a whole lot about, but it's interesting to me. Mozart, for example, was obviously a well-known composer in his own right; but he also did some musical ghostwriting for other wealthy patrons. He actually wrote scores for these people, and they got to claim them as their own! **They were able to give the impression that they were great, gifted composers... and yet it was *Mozart* who was actually doing the composing for them.** He didn't get any of that credit, just the money. He got enough credit for his own work, apparently.

Most of the music you hear on the radio these days, particularly in popular categories, is actually ghostwritten. Sometimes the performers give credit to the person who wrote the song, but it depends on the situation. While there are certainly exceptions, in most cases the music isn't written by the performer at all. **Maybe the person looks good and can sing well, but doesn't have the talent to *write* music—so they, or their managers, will have someone else do it.** That's another option, then: if you're gifted as a musician, or as a writer in the musical sense, then you can sell your songs as a musical ghostwriter.

Finally, fiction can also be profitable. You can take someone's basic ideas for a mystery, romance, or science fiction novel (or whatever), and do the writing for them.

Think about all that. You can make up to $28,000, on average, for ghostwriting a book (according to Ghostwriters, Inc.). Of course, you can also get paid a lot less, too; and realize that as you're starting out, you're *not* going to get paid the big bucks. **But you can make a lot of money even part-time as a writer, and you'll get better as you gain experience and hone your skills. So get your name out there.** Become more popular in the world of ghostwriting. **Once you reach a certain level of notoriety, your business can run on autopilot; all you do is the writing.** You don't need to advertise anymore, because word of mouth kicks in. People refer you to their friends, their clients, their colleagues. This is where our ghostwriter Floyd is right now. As he himself would tell you, it's rare for him to have to go out and do any marketing at this point—but he's always ready to hustle whenever he has to, so you should be, too.

Just keep the writing coming. Keep having fun. Live the lifestyle you've always wanted. **Live the dream of being a writer, and get paid nice sums of money to write words that other people get to take credit for.** Now, if you're looking for fame, maybe ghostwriting isn't the right field for you. But if you don't mind other people getting the credit for your words, and you don't mind being famous among the people who need the kind of writing that you can provide, perhaps being a ghostwriter is a good career choice for you, and can be a fun way to make a lifetime of profits.

A Possible Path

I hope that this chapter throws some new light on the world of writing, offering a perspective that you may not have thought about before. **The bottom line is, if you want to get paid to write, there's no excuse for you not to!** I don't mean to be offensive here, but look: there are so many ways you can do it. And no, you may not get the big bucks right away—but that's true of any field of endeavor, isn't it? **You may have to keep working at it, but keep in mind that you *can* start earning even as you continue to learn and sharpen your skills. Market yourself.** Make an effort to show people what you can do. Eventually, if you do good, professional work, word of mouth will kick in. People will talk about you. **The demand really is incredible, and the work is straightforward, creative, challenging... and lucrative.**

It can be as simple as pretending you're Larry King, interviewing a few people, and writing up what they say. Or you could do what Floyd Largent does for us: take printed transcripts from recordings, and polish them up. Floyd's been working for us for so long now that he understands so much about the type of marketing information we provide that he has free rein to fill in the gaps and smooth over whatever he hears. **It's the same benefit you'll have when you have long-term clients and come to understand the kind of material that they want you to ghostwrite for them, and as they gain confidence in you.** It becomes an excellent working relationship that's born out of respect, one that can continue for many years.

Remember, all you need is a handful of good clients who will continue to work with you for many years in order to have a thriving business where you're getting paid to do what you love to do. **When you become a client of our Get Paid to Write coaching program, we'll provide all the sales material you need to get out there, start finding these prospects, and show them just how beneficial you can be to them.**

The more clients you bring on board, the more your confidence is going to increase. **Don't let your fear stop you.** With something new, there's always going to be a little fear involved. **The more you do it, though, the more confidence you're going to build.** Don't forget that even the highest-paid ghostwriters started at the very bottom before working their way up. As I like to say, a big shot is just a little shot that kept right on shooting! You're always going to be more confident on the fifth project you do than you were the previous four. By the time you get to the 10th project, your confidence is going to take over. You simply have to realize that it's going to be a little uncomfortable before it does become comfortable. **But once you settle in, once you do enough of it, once it does become comfortable, then you'll have developed the skills that are necessary.** You'll be getting paid the big bucks.

You'll have earned those big bucks, too, because you had the courage to persist where so many people did not. It's human nature for people to just give up as soon as they run into any obstacles whatsoever. Don't. The demand for ghostwriters (and copywriters) is absolutely incredible. **You *can* fill that demand and make a lot of money for yourself, help your clients a great deal, and get paid to do what you love.**

That's the name of the game.

Chapter Eight:

Introduction to Information Marketing

In this chapter, **I'm going to discuss the third and final way that you can get paid to write. This is one of the most exciting, if not *the* most exciting, of all three, and it can potentially make you millions of dollars.** Even if you don't want to make millions, you can easily make a solid six-figure income by following the methods I've outlined here—especially since I know for a fact that average people can make millions this way. **I'm living proof!** You see, 23 years ago my wife and I took just $300 and used all three of the methods that I've described in this book to build that investment into over $140 million in total revenue so far. I don't say that to brag on us, but to prove the viability of the three methods I'm teaching, at least when you combine them as we have.

I've talked about copywriting and ghostwriting in other chapters. **The third way to get paid to write is through information marketing.** When we first started our company, the sign in front of the building read "self-publishing." That's what we called it back then. **But this field encompasses so much more than just self-publishing!** When I think of self-publishing nowadays, I think of books, which actually have the least amount of perceived value of all information products. They still serve a valuable purpose in your overall value mix, but I want you to get your eyes off self-publishing as such and stop thinking about books that retail for under $20, usually, or definitely under $30. **Instead, start thinking of information products that can retail for hundreds or thousands of dollars.**

When you start thinking of information marketing in relation to the ideas I'm going to share with you in the rest of this book, you'll see that you really *can* get thousands of dollars for some information products. **The reason that people are happy to pay you so much is because of the high perceived value of what you're offering in exchange for their money.** It has nothing to do with what it costs you, though, so keep that in mind. We'll give you some very clear real-world examples from our past history outlining why that's true.

Now: although this book is called *Get Paid to Write*, realize also that some of the information programs and products that you can put together may not involve much writing at all. **Consider, for instance, video DVDs.** One of the products I'm going to talk about later involves you or someone else getting in front of a camera. **You could write a script for them, and they could work from that; or they could just work under your direction.** Still, there's almost always writing involved... or at least, there is for me. I can't work without notes at the very minimum, so I'm always doing a lot of writing.

For instance, we publish a lot of audio programs. Sure, those programs are of us just talking; but we still do a lot of writing in the form of note-taking before we ever get in front of the microphone, and there's often a lot of advanced reading required just to research our topics. **So yes, some of what I'll discuss in this section goes beyond mere writing. In addition to audio products, we also do a lot of seminars—the seminar being another profitable type of information marketing**

product. Most of our seminars vary in price from a few hundred to a few thousand dollars, and we've sold a few for up to $6,700. Again, that form of information marketing doesn't necessarily involve much writing, but you'll still need to do extensive note-taking, at the bare minimum.

So yes, information marketing does involve more than just writing. You've got to think outside the box just a little; in fact, I'd like you to think holistically as an information marketer. **I promise you, writing *does* play a big role in any information marketing effort.**

Now, somebody can really only teach you what they know; otherwise
it's just a bunch of theory. So I thought I'd start by giving you some stories from our own past, using them to illustrate certain principles behind information marketing.

Production Cost Does Not Equal Value

My wife Eileen and I started our parent company in September 1988; our first publication was a little booklet called *Dialing for Dollars*. Actually, it was more like a brochure than a booklet. Honestly, it was a junky little publication: cheaply done, poorly written, filled with typographical errors, not laid out very well. **And yet it was the seed that grew into a business that ultimately generated over $10 million in gross revenue for us in our first five years as entrepreneurs.**

We went on to make over $140 million in total revenue within our first 23 years, which is where we are now. It all evolved from this little booklet, which showed people how they could make money with a telephone answering machine. You recorded messages to replace a live salesperson, to sell these special publications that we put together. People bought our booklet, and it showed them how we had four other publications they could sell—publications that were specifically aimed at advertising in newspapers. For instance, we had a book on making money with garage sales that went into the Garage Sales section. We had a book on getting government jobs which our distributors advertised in the Help Wanted section, and so on. That's how we started.

So we basically started with five publications: our flagship, *Dialing for Dollars*—which was basically a poorly written brochure—and four other publications that our distributors could buy wholesale and sell retail. Four years later, we had 37 different publications they could sell. **We just kept expanding on the concept, eventually adding** *Dialing for Dollars Part 2* **and** *Dialing for Dollars Part 3.*

By the way, that concept of using a recorded message to do part or all of the selling for you is still alive and well. We still use it every single day, only now we use voicemail instead of answering machines. It's a good, viable idea—and with that tiny publication that cost us about fifty cents to produce, we parlayed that idea into millions. As I told you when I opened this chapter, **that's one of the benefits of selling information: it's cheap to produce, and yet often has an extremely high perceived value.** Right out of the gate we were making thousands of dollars every month, just by selling this booklet and then working with our dealers as they ordered these four publications that they sold.

We were so proud of ourselves. **I was 28 years old at the time, and my wife was 30—and until then, we had never**

made any substantial money in our whole lives. We had struggled financially for so many years, and all of a sudden we were making thousands of dollars a month, and we were feeling really good about it! Of course, some people didn't get it, which really hurt us. I'll never forget the day we went over to my Dad's house, and showed *Dialing for Dollars* to him and his wife. We weren't necessarily bragging, but we were very happy with our business and what we were accomplishing.

Now, my Dad was married to a lady who was very, very smart. She flipped through it, and she saw that it wasn't written very well. It was thin, too; and she looked at us and asked us how much we were selling it for. At that time, it was selling for $12.95, though we kept building it up and beefing it up and making it bigger, until eventually we were selling it for $29. Well, she knew that we couldn't have paid more than a couple of quarters to print it... and when she found out how much we were selling it for, she literally tossed it across the room and said, "This is shit." Pardon my language, but that's exactly what she said; those are her words, not mine.

Of course, I was very upset. This was our baby! **This was our pride and joy, we were proud of our business, and it was bringing in some good money!** Needless today, her reaction caused a lot of problems. My Dad got mad at her, I didn't speak to her for a few years, and of course we quit going over to their house and all that.

That was over 20 years ago. Now I'm a little older, a little wiser, and a little more mature, and sure, I can see where she was coming from now. **The real problem was that she didn't understand our marketplace.** She didn't understand that this opportunity market we were serving was filled with other small publishing companies like ours, companies that were producing programs that were not proven in any way and didn't make any money at all. She didn't know that we had customers who were making thousands of dollars a month with our program by that point. Before long, we had people who were making $10,000-20,000 a month. **Eventually, we had people who were making $30,000, $40,000, even $50,000 a month with the basic secret in our little booklet.** We even had one guy out of Provo, Utah who was doing $5 million a year in sales before he cut us off and stared producing his own publications! But all that my stepmother saw was that we were selling something that cost us fifty cents for $12.95... and she thought we were cheating people. She looked at the quality of it, and it turned her off.

But she was judging it as an outsider. Our customers loved it. We literally had people driving in from four or five states away just to meet us in person and shake our hands, to thank us for producing something that really changed their lives and turned things around for them. So the cost of something has very little to do with how much you can sell it for. **What matters— the *only* thing that matters—is how much value it has in the mind of the customer.**

Keep Growing – And Keep Focusing on Your Customers

If you really want to succeed, you also need to keep expanding, giving your customers more and more of what they want. With *Dialing for Dollars*, we started with four publications for our dealers, and ultimately ended up with 37. We produced a lot of other things for them, too. **We kept focusing on them.** You see, quite often people are so confused when they start in business that they don't know what they're going to sell. They spend so much time worrying about that and wallowing in confusion that they finally throw their arms up in the air and say "Forget it!" They just give up. **But if you simply focus on your customers, by first giving them one product they love and then creating other related products for them, you can thrive.**

Our next huge break came after we'd been in business for a couple of years. This was the first product that we actually made over a million dollars on, and it started with such a simple idea—one that I got while I was in the shower. That's where I've gotten a lot of ideas over the years, for some strange reason; don't ask me why. Sometimes I'll sit in the shower for an hour, just thinking.

Anyway: we had hired a consultant named Russ von Hoelscher, who at the time had been in the business for over 20 years. We used to pay him $2,500 plus airfare to fly from South California to Wichita to spend a weekend at our home. We'd pick him up on a Friday afternoon and drop him off on a Sunday afternoon, and take good care of him in between. **He'd spend that entire weekend advising us and helping us develop product ideas for our customers.** Among other things, he helped us do our very first seminar, on September 22, 1990. That was all him, just working with us, trying to encourage us, trying to help us give our customers more, more, more.

We had had him over to the house probably three different times. Well, one day I was in the shower thinking about our customers, and what we might do for them and create for them, and I thought: "Look, why don't we just get Russ to come down here to our house again? **We'll pay him his regular fee, only this time we'll record the entire conversation. And then we'll**

**sell that product to our customers by telling the story about
how we paid him $2,500 to come and spend a weekend with
us, and that they can get the best of the best of our
recordings for just $195."**

We figured that our customers could instantly see the
wisdom of spending $195 to get something extremely valuable
that we had paid $2,500 for—and they did. **They just loved it.**
As I mentioned in an earlier chapter, I spent several months
working on that sales letter. **We sent it out to our customers,
and $1.3 million came rushing in.** And it was just such a
simple idea! We had a little $50 Radio Shack recorder; we just
stuck it right there on the dining room table, and asked Russ all
the questions that we knew our customers would want to know.
These were the same questions we had when we were first
getting started.

Not only did the sales take off like a rocket, people gave us
so many compliments on that program. They didn't see that as a
cheap product at all, although it was actually poorly produced. I
mean, you could hear our coffee cups clanking in the
background, and sometimes you could hear us talking with our
mouths full of pastry. **It was cheaply done, no doubt about it:
and yet to the customers, it represented real value, and it
ultimately generated over a million dollars for us.**

So what's instructional about that story? **Simply that you
have to start with a really good idea, and stay focused on
your customers.** You have to tell a great story, build that value
up, make them see the value, and make it all about them.
Because that's really what that product was about—and the truth
is, that's what all our products are about. **The only time we fail
to make money is when we get away from the customers and**

what they really want.

As I write this, we had a phenomenal tele-seminar last week: we did $75,000 worth of business on a 70-minute session. I spent a lot of time coming up with ideas for that tele-seminar, but in the end, Chris Lakey trumped those ideas with some of his own. **Why? Because his ideas were more focused on what the customers wanted than mine were.** So we tossed my ideas, and his became the theme for our entire session. We did $75,000 worth of business in a 70-minute period thanks to Chris being in tune with exactly what the customers really, truly wanted.

Now, it sounds like common sense to give customers exactly what they want; and **yet we all sometimes make the mistake of trying to sell people the things we want to sell them rather than the things they want to buy.** Keep what *they* want firmly in mind.

Information Marketing = Freedom

At M.O.R.E., Inc , we serve the opportunity marketplace. But if you back up just a little, you see that we're really information marketers. **We've identified a group of people who are interested in something, and we've set out to give them what they want: information on making money from home.** We help people by getting them involved in business opportunities, and yet, we're not selling investment advice, or franchises, or anything like that. **People can use the information we provide to create businesses for themselves, or not. It's up to them.** We do have some services that we offer people, but **our core business is selling people money-making information.** The information we sell takes all kinds of shapes and sizes, and the details change over time, but it remains our core business. Similarly, we've used a variety of different formats to communicate that information. For example, the book you're reading now started out as an audio program; and we've also used newsletters, DVDs, and video as formats for our products.

There's a great book on information marketing by our friend Dan Kennedy that offers an excellent summary of how to make money as an information marketer. I'm going to include a passage from that book here, because I think he did a good job of describing why information marketing is so powerful. **Here's what Dan has to say:**

> **No other business offers you the kinds of fascinating and lucrative opportunities that information marketing does.** You can pursue things that interest you, travel or not travel as you please. But if you do please, legitimately make it tax deductible. **Operate globally from your kitchen table and place yourself in the Top One Percent of Income Earner's Club in a short a time as one year.** You can become a celebrity or remain anonymous, as you prefer. **You can begin humbly or audaciously.**
>
> One of the people I first studied when I was starting 30 years ago had begun by selling a $5 booklet about ridding your garden of gophers, via tiny classified ads in rural newspapers and farm magazines. **One of the most recent information businesses I helped launch started out selling a $40,000 coaching program.**
>
> **You can work when you please, where you please, as you please.** You can have some employees, a lot of

employees, or no employees. You can outsource whatever you aren't good at or interested in. You can personally interact with your customers through tele-seminars, seminars, and coaching programs, or you can make millions without ever meeting a single one of your customers face-to-face.

I could go on and on with this long list of flexibility, but the point is this: **You make the rules.** You bend this business to your preferences and you need sacrifice nothing for enormous financial success.

For me, this sums up everything about why information marketing is such a great business to be in. **Now think about that: you can pursue things that interest you.** In the information marketing business, your information is whatever you want it to be. If you happen to like gardening, you can write about gardening. If you're interested in golfing, you can write an information product about golfing. If you're interested in being a good stay-at-home mom or a good musician— whatever you're interested in—that can be a business that you pursue. **You get to decide.**

If you like to travel, you could travel as a business and create an information product that's related to traveling. You can even deduct it from your taxes, since the government allows you that when you're making money on something. See your accountant for specific rules and regulations of course, but the point is that you can turn your interest into a fun, travel-related business, if you care to.

As an information marketer, you can operate anywhere in the world, whether on vacation or at home. **You can do**

whatever you want and be wherever you want, and still be making money. You're not tied to a desk or a local storefront. **You can be a celebrity in your marketplace, or you can remain completely anonymous.** Some information marketers use a pen name, so no one even knows who they are. Others put their name out there in public. You can also decide to do things on a small scale or a grand scale; you control the volume, so to speak, of the business you create. If you want just a little bit of money, you crank down the volume. If you want a lot of money, you crank it up. **Once the system is working, you can control the amount of money that comes into your business based on the amount of hours and energy you decide to put into it.**

Do you want to interact with your customers, or do you prefer to maintain your privacy? Your choice. We prefer the former option ourselves, and it's certainly a requirement for anyone who has a public information marketing business. **People who sell coaching programs, seminars, and live events have to be out there interacting with people on a regular basis; there's no way around that.** They're constantly in front of their marketplace, talking to people all the time. **On the other hand, some information marketers have never met a single one of their customers.** They do business by mail or the Internet. They never answer the phone personally; if someone has a question, they email support. Sure, they might do some email correspondence, but they've never talked on the phone to anybody. They don't like to interact personally with clients, so they've never heard one of their client's voices, much less met them face-to-face. And they still make huge amounts of money.

As Dan emphasized, *you* make the rules, and you bend this business to your preferences. So what do you want your information marketing business to be? The good news is, it can be just about whatever you want it to be. Granted, there are some legal, moral, and ethical bounds to business; so if you want to avoid penalties and fines, and possibly prison time, you'll play within the rules. **So we're not talking about a situation where *anything* goes; but within those rather broad boundaries, your information marketing business can be whatever you dream it to be.**

That's one of the things we love about information marketing. When we set out to provide a product or a service to our clients, we do our best to determine what they want the very most, and we try to give them that. **We're keenly aware that most of our clients want to make money from home in a business that's very passive, very hands-off.** They don't want to have a lot of interaction with clients. They don't want to have to talk on the phone all day, and they don't really want to put in a lot of hours. So we know what our clients are looking for.

But there's a lot of opportunity for variance within that broader strategy, and we can take a lot of creative license with how we deliver it. That's where our ability to give them what they want the way that we want to give it to them comes into play. **For example, we decided to first offer this *Get Paid to Write* product as an audio program. You're reading it now because we also decided to turn at least some of this material into a book.** I could have decided to make this a book from the very beginning. I could have decided to deliver this content via a newsletter that people subscribe to for an annual fee, producing it over several months or years. I could even have done it on DVD, simply by sitting in front of a video camera and sharing my thoughts with you. I could have presented this material at a live event, with hundreds of people in the audience.

As you can see, within the intention of providing this valuable information to our clients, **we have the creative license to decide the format that's going to take.** That means that we can do what we like the best, using whatever venue or venues are optimal for the information we're trying to impart.

As it happens, we love producing audio programs. It's easy for Chris Lakey and me to get on the phone and spend an hour talking and sharing what we're excited about with our clients. That doesn't mean that we don't put a lot of work, energy, and heart into what we're doing; but **it *is* relatively easy to delivery this information in spoken-word format compared to presenting the same information in written format, directly as a book.** That's why we chose to start with an audio format for this particular project. We're already converting it into other formats; you've got the book version in your hands, and we may make it into a series of newsletters. But originally, we chose to deliver this information in the audio format.

Let's look at another form of freedom that information marketing allows: **the freedom to live the lifestyle that you prefer.** If you want to be on the beach most of the time, you can relocate your information marketing business to Miami. You can even live in a foreign country, or have a second home, spending half the year where it's warm and half the year where it's cooler. **Whatever lifestyle you choose to live, whatever dream you envision for yourself and for your family, information marketing can help you create that, because you *do* have choices.** You don't have to work wherever your employer tells you to work. A lot of people relocate their families and their lives not because they want to move, but because their employer says they have to move or lose their job.

No more of that with information marketing: you can live anywhere. You can work from home, or out of an office if you want to. **You have the ultimate control, because it's your business—and it can be whatever you want it to be.**

Some Cautions About Information Marketing

While information marketing isn't necessarily the same as writing for pay (unlike ghostwriting or copywriting), **the most successful information marketers nonetheless have a good grasp on marketing via writing.** They need to, because most information marketers sell their products and services by writing sales copy about them in some format or another. **If you're in the mail order business, for example, you have to write sales letters to sell your information product; if you're selling online, you write website copy.** Maybe you sell via brochures or other print literature, or maybe you sell via classified ads or display ads. **Almost all the ways you can use to sell an information product will include writing.** So if you're serious about information marketing, you're going to have to be serious about at least learning the basics behind copywriting.

One of the things that we always teach here at M.O.R.E., Inc. is that it's important not to delegate your marketing. You can delegate lots of other stuff safely: you can have someone answer the phones for you, do your customer service, or ship your products out. But don't delegate your marketing. Take care of that yourself. **For information marketers, that usually means, among other things, learning how to write sales copy.** So the principles I've already outlined in the chapters on copywriting will certainly become important to you as an information marketer. **You'll want to learn to write your own ads and sales letters because you want total control over that part of the process.**

At the beginning of your business, your most difficult decision will be to find a profitable field to work in. We've found the business opportunity market to be extremely lucrative for us, and I would imagine that there are other marketplaces that are just as lucrative, maybe more so. **Others don't have much capacity for profit, sadly, especially if the subject is mundane or there's simply too much information available for free on the Internet.** The Internet has changed business quite a bit, and the information marketing industry has seen a lot of transformations because of it. Now, don't get me wrong: there are plenty of opportunities *because* of the Internet, so don't let that discourage you. But if your business is based on something people can get for free by Googling it, then you'd better have a really good reason why they should pay you for it.

For example: just the other day Chris was looking for help on how to do something on his computer, so he Googled it—and quickly found a website that gave him an easy answer on how to do what he was trying to do. So if you're trying to get into the business of helping people fix that particular problem on their computer, they're probably not going to pay you for a report, since it's so easy to get that same information for free on the Internet. **You need to go beyond what people can get for free. Make it bigger, make it better. Package it differently.** Do something to make it so that they might want to pay for that information, even though they *could* get it free.

So what do you choose as your specialty? As with any other form of writing or information exchange, **one of the**

easiest ways to get into the information business is to sell something you know about. If you know how to do something in particular—fix a car, make origami figures, cook, whatever—you can write about it or record an audio program about it, and sell it via a website. That's the easiest way to get started: to think of a marketplace you're already a part of and familiar with, and turn that into your business.

Again, just be careful that you're not being too simplistic, that you're not answering a question that people can get the answer to for free via any other source. **What you really need is something that's not obvious, a topic where you're providing more than what they could easily get, where you're doing all the research for them.** Let's say that, yes, they could probably find an answer on their own, but it would take them six weeks and a lot of frustration to do so. If that's the case, you've got a viable model to work from. But if they can just Google something and get a quick answer, you're probably not going to be able to use it as the foundation of a business that will make you the kind of money that you want to make. Just be aware of that as you're considering what to do.

The Creativity Aspect

Writing and the other forms of communication used in direct marketing are inextricably linked. In my case, the more I write about a subject, the better I am at getting up in front of a room full of people and talking about it, or recording an audio program on the subject, or even discussing it in front of a video camera—and there's nothing that I hate worse than a camera in my face. **Having written a lot about a subject means that I can freely and confidently express my knowledge through all** those other media.

You must understand that this is a very creative business in all its formats. Most writers choose their craft because they love the creative aspects of it—the artistic part of being a writer. Well, information marketing is a very creative endeavor as well, in large part because it's whatever you want it to be. **You can do so many different things, and that's the essence of creativity: combining all these different ideas in a new way, and developing something new as a result.** From the information marketing perspective, this allows you to deliver tremendous value.

As I've already emphasized, in order to make any money in this field, you have to choose a lucrative marketplace first; but you also have to choose a marketplace that you have some passion for. One of the things that all books on creative writing tell you is to **"write what you know."** You've probably already heard that rule. Now, it's just a general rule; you don't have to be a murderer to write mystery novels, or a time traveler to write science fiction. But when it comes to information marketing, you most assuredly have to write what you know. **If you don't know much about a particular subject, then either learn as you go, or hire experts to actually deliver the content.**

We've done plenty of that. We've even produced a program on an aspect of making money that I know and care very little about. In fact, I pretty much hate most aspects of this type of information marketing, but because our customers are interested in it, we produced a huge 50-hour audio program a while back— on something I still don't know much about. That subject was real estate. If there's one money-making subject I hate more than anything else, it's making money with real estate. It's just too complicated, too confusing for me. I just can't do the math, no matter how hard I try. But this product wasn't for me; it was something my customers wanted, so we gave it to them. **I can't emphasize how important it is to forget what** *you* **want and focus entirely on your customers.** So what did we do? We got a bunch of experts together, and we interviewed them. We played Larry King. The first few interviews we did were very uncomfortable for me, but after about 12 or 13 of them, I started getting into it and knew what to ask.

The point is, you don't actually have to be the one who's delivering the content in order to produce an extremely valuable program that people will love. You can get creative in the presentation, and reach out to other people who can provide the information you want to present. **Just think outside the box, and be very creative.**

Our Big Secret

All that said, the best advice that I can give you, the one secret that has made us more money than anything else, is simply this: **you need to know your chosen marketplace inside and out.** In our case, we were already very active members of our marketplace, so we understood nearly all aspects of it. I've recounted elsewhere in this book how sick I was of all the unskilled jobs I'd held over the years. I didn't go to college, so I couldn't get a "decent" job. All I knew how to do was a higher grade of manual labor, and I hated every minute of it.

So for years, I sent away for every money-making plan and program I could get my hands on. I was an opportunity enthusiast—even an opportunity junkie. I couldn't get enough of these programs. You see them advertised in the backs of tabloids and magazines like *Popular Mechanics* and *Popular Science*. **That's the market we serve, basically: the opportunity market.** God only knows, there's a whole bunch of people in this market, just thousands and thousands of tiny dealers selling all kinds of stuff. I was buying from all these companies, so my name ended up on all their mailing lists, and they started sending me offers without me asking.

At one point, every last available dollar that I had went to these products, to the point where I occasionally wrote hot checks for them. I'm not real proud of that, but, hey, at the time I thought, "Well, if the program really works for me, I'll pay them back." I justified it, rationalized it, and minimized my bad behavior.

When I met my wife, Eileen, she was working as a cashier at a filling station, making minimum wage, and yet she was extremely ambitious. Like me, she wanted a better life. She had big dreams and big plans. I met her when she was 30 years old and recently divorced. **She saw my ambition, and I showed her all these programs I was buying.** She laughed at some of the programs I bought—some of them were really ridiculous— but she didn't laugh at me for buying them. **Instead, she helped me pick out the really good ones, and she helped me study those programs. Ultimately, we created a program that was uniquely ours;** that was the *Dialing for Dollars* program that I described earlier in the chapter. **It was a $300 investment.** We ran a small ad in a couple of money-making magazines, and that investment quickly turned into an income of $500 a day. **Then we met Russ von Hoelscher; he worked with us, and we went on to bring in millions of dollars.**

Little did I know when we got started that, as the kiddies

say, "It takes one to know one." You've heard that a million times, and you've probably said it yourself when you were a kid. **Well, it *does* take one to know one.** When we started in this market in September 1988, the customers we were attracting were exactly like me. They were also opportunity junkies, addicted to buying the kinds of programs that ended up selling. That was a good thing for us, because we knew all the problems those people were faced with. **Without even realizing it, we instinctively understood the people in this market.** I thought there were maybe thousands of us at the time... but it turns out that there are millions, and most of us just can't get enough of these products.

In this market—in any rabid market—you get on mailing lists, and everybody buys and sells and trades your name. **Eventually you're on hundreds of different lists,** so your mailbox is packed full of offers every day. That happened to me, and I was studying those offers. I intimately understood these people without even realizing it, and such an understanding of the target marketplace is necessary if you really want to succeed. **I was lucky that I chose the right marketplace, because I really had no idea, at the time, just how lucrative it was. But it was also a market that interested me.** I was interested in it back then, and 23 years later, I'm every bit as much interested in it, if not more so. Although I now understand some of the dirty, darker sides of the market that I didn't back then, I still love the market.

So the best advice that I can give you, based on our past success, is to simply find a market that you really love, something that you really enjoy, as long as it's lucrative. And realize that some markets work better for information products than others. **Find out what other people are selling, so you know what's worth pursuing.** Without even realizing it, that's exactly what I was doing during my buying phase: I knew a lot about what other companies were selling because I was buying it. The companies I was buying all that stuff from ended up being my competitors, though I really didn't think that way back then. **I still don't focus on the competition, actually, except that I try to stay in tune with what people are buying and what they really want.**

And keep this in mind: even if you choose a great marketplace and get to know it intimately, you'll still mess things up sometimes. Even when you've become an expert, and think you're in tune with what people want, you can still make errors—like I did last week with that tele-seminar, the one I mentioned in an earlier part of this chapter. Thank goodness Chris came along and pointed out that I was going at it from the wrong angle, then proceeded to give me the solution. **So realize that even when you think you know it all, there's still plenty to learn... and sometimes you can still forget things here and there.**

The Low-Risk Factor

Overnight successes rarely happen in any field of endeavor. There are plenty of entrepreneurs out there who are huge successes now, but who missed the boat with earlier businesses and marketplaces. So as far as information marketing goes, don't think that you have to get it right the first time. **Be willing to take chances and fail forward, if you must... because compared to other types of businesses, failing in the information marketing field can be very cheap.** There's usually very little cash tied up in your business, so you generally risk very little. **If things aren't going right, you can quickly change gears to enter a new marketplace, and you're really not out much of anything.**

Remember, we launched what became M.O.R.E., Inc. with $300. **Admittedly it was our last $300 at the time; but if it hadn't gone as planned, we wouldn't have been out any more than that.** No doubt we would have gone in another direction and refused to give up until we found something that worked for us.

So you can spend a few hundred or, maybe, a few thousand dollars, trying to find out if the marketplace you're interested in is going to be profitable or not. Of course, that can be somewhat painful, but most people who lose a few thousand dollars learning something consider it a good education, not a total loss. That's how you have to look at information marketing. And remember: although a particular marketplace may have a long track record of people who have been successful selling information to that market, that doesn't necessarily mean you'll find success with your product. **But if you know the marketplace exists, you can refuse to give up, and keep trying to find a different angle, a different product or service, that the marketplace *does* want to buy.** And because information is so easy to produce in its various forms, that risk remains small.

If we wanted to enter a new marketplace—something that we've not been in yet, but that we know exists and is profitable—**the first step in creating our offer would probably be to write a sales letter.** Most of what we do is done through direct mail, so a sales letter tends to be our first step in almost every case. **Then we'd rent a mailing list of people in that marketplace, and we would send them our offer.** Hopefully, we would get leads in response to the letter; and **then we would do our best to turn those leads into paying customers.** If the whole thing worked as we hoped it would, we would have the start of a good, additional revenue stream for our business.

Even if the idea didn't succeed immediately, the results might be good enough for us to go back to the drawing board and retool it a little. We could try to come up with a better offer, something that they responded to more readily. Maybe we didn't completely match the right offer to the right marketplace in our initial effort, or we didn't do enough research, or the marketplace wasn't big enough. **Whatever the case, we wouldn't be out a whole lot of money, no matter what.** Even if it all failed miserably, we might have spent a few thousand dollars on it, no more.

Compared to a traditional brick-and-mortar business, or compared to buying an expensive franchise, the risks here are very, very minimal. Think about your average franchise: you might spend $50,000 or $100,000 just to get your franchise license. If you start your business up and a year or two later it's just not going well, you're out of luck. You've sunk so much money into it. You really hate to give up on it, and yet the time has come to do so. The customers aren't coming in the door. You're exhausting all your life savings, and maybe you owe the bank a bunch of money... and it's time to call it quits. Maybe you sank a quarter of a million dollars into this failed business.

It's just not that way with information marketing. Oh, sure—you can spend a lot of money getting your message to that marketplace, especially if you're doing things like direct mail.

So it *can* be very expensive, but your startup costs to find out
if you've got a winner are very minimal. You spend the big
money only when you really believe or know it will be
profitable. First, you can do something like mail a thousand
direct mail sales letters, and get an idea of whether you have a
winner or not. At the very least, you'll find out whether you
need to test some more, or change the whole offer, or whatever.

   **Similarly, on the Internet you can spend a small
amount of money for some pay-per-click advertising.** You
can set up a website essentially for free, if you've got an
existing server to host it on. **You can write a sales letter and
sell something online without spending very much money at
all.** You don't have to risk a lot of money finding your success
in information marketing.

A Question of Value

   **Once you do make a hit, once you determine how to
reach the right kind of marketplace with the kind of
information that they want the most, information
marketing can be a very lucrative way to make money.**
Earlier, I quoted from Dan Kennedy's book on information
marketing, and he shares the example of a client who was
selling a $40,000 coaching program. **So you can charge an
enormous amount of money for information, and people
will line up to pay for it.** Dan doesn't say who was paying
$40,000 for that coaching program, but the right kind of
information to the right marketplace is worth more than gold—
and people *will* pay for that.

   I know of a specific investment strategy newsletter that
sells for $5,000 per year. For the clients interested in that

subject, $5000 a year is a steal. You might not think so... but if that's the case, then the newsletter isn't targeting you. Think about that; it just passes you by if you're not interested in it. **But if the information is something you desperately want or need, you would pay almost anything for it.** If your child was sick with cancer and you knew there was a cure, you'd pay anything to buy that cure. If it was necessary, you'd sell your house; you'd sell a kidney. You'd do whatever you could to acquire that information that would help to save your child.

Marketplaces are like that. **If a person perceives that the information you have to offer is of great value to them, they'll pay a fortune for it.** It doesn't matter if it's written on a napkin from a restaurant, or if it's printed in a book, or if it's provided in audio format—it's the information and what it reveals that matters, *not* the cost of the material that it's printed or recorded on. A CD costs a buck, but a CD with the right information on it could sell for $1,000 or more.

A piece of paper is worth a few cents at most. But what's written on that paper could be worth a fortune to somebody who wants that information badly enough. Don't forget my story of my Dad's wife throwing our first little *Dialing for Dollars* publication across the room and saying "This is shit." She had absolutely no idea what it was worth to the people in our marketplace—how it directly addressed their frustrations and their challenges. **They were more than willing to spend $12.95 on the publication, which was a steal compared to what they were spending on other things.** If they liked the idea, they could then invest in it—and many people did.

She didn't see any real value in it because it wasn't meant for people like her. She didn't understand the entire basis of it.

But other people saw tremendous value in that program. *It's all about perception of value.* There are plenty of things you can do in the packaging of your product to give it a higher perceived value... and that's what I'll talk about in the next chapter. **I'll go over a list of 40 different types of information products, and will share with you the details of how you can significantly increase your overall profitability by changing the way that you deliver the information.**

I hope that this entry level discussion has piqued your interest, and you're excited about all of this. I urge you to go on to the next chapter right now!

Pen-And-Paper Options

In this chapter, **I'll begin outlining my list of 40 different types of information products that you can create, within which there are many subtle variations.** Remember: to some degree, all of this is just limited by your imagination, so the list of 40 isn't absolute. Originally, these items came out of a book called *The Official Get Rich Guide to Information Marketing* published by Dan Kennedy, Bill Glazer, and Robert Skrob for the Information Marketing Association, which we've been members of right from the very beginning. **We recommend that you look into the IMA and consider membership yourself.** You can find them on the Internet. **And if you're really interested in information marketing, then get their book!** It's going to cost you a maximum of $24.95 in hardback, less in paper. You can even get a Kindle edition on Amazon.com for less than 10 bucks. You'll see that we've even got a chapter in it!

Now, one of the cool things about information marketing is that it can be whatever you want it to be. An information product can take many different forms, so there are a lot of different things to discuss when it comes to the types of information you sell. **In this chapter, we're going to start with a list of 15 paper-and-ink products, and then move on to other areas like audio and Internet products in later chapters.**

Most of these pen-and-ink products we've done ourselves here at M.O.R.E., Inc., and those we haven't, we've seen other people do. **My hope is that at least one of these product types will strike a chord and get you excited, so you'll start thinking about how you can put your own products together.** Who knows? Maybe by the time you're done reading this chapter, you'll be on your way to creating your first information product.

The Product Types

The FIRST type of paper-and-ink I'd like to discuss is reports. Usually, a report is a short document, 1-8 pages long, focused on a specific topic. The length depends on how much information you need to impart. Sometimes you can be as concise as one page. Usually it requires more, sometimes quite a bit more, to reveal it properly. I've seen reports as long as 20 pages, and a very few as long as 50 pages—or even longer. If it gets any longer than that, it's really a book. **The point is, it's the information that makes the report valuable, not necessarily the length.** So you can have just a few pages, but still reveal valuable information that's worth a lot of money to somebody. It doesn't matter how short your report is if that's the case.

NUMBER TWO is tip sheets. Tip sheets are usually shorter than reports: typically they're one page long, very specialized, with no fluff. **A tip sheet is very technical—a detailed how-to on whatever it is that you're providing the tip on.** That makes it valuable to the person receiving it, so you can sell than information for a high price. **Needless to say, the kind of information you reveal must be something they can't get anywhere else—not by Googling, or by doing research in the**

library or elsewhere. This is highly specific information, very straightforward, without any filler at all. It's straight to the point.

NUMBER THREE: manuals, usually published in loose-leaf notebook or spiral-bound format. We've published a lot of three-ring binder manuals—some smaller, some larger, some that are as big as traditional books. They're expandable, if you like, and give you a lot more room to say what it is that you want to say than a report does. **A manual is generally detailed and technical in nature, regarding something specific that people need to learn, acting as a fulfillment for the information they purchased.**

NUMBER FOUR: books. Not much explanation needed there; a book is a book. You're reading one now. You've probably bought hundreds of them in your lifetime. **A book can contain the same information as a manual, only bound in a permanent format.**

NUMBER FIVE: a boxed set of books. If you have a collection of your own books, you could box them up and sell them as a set. Or, you could create an official boxed set for a collection of books that other people have written. You're just the one who organized them. Maybe you've acquired the rights to distribute them at a discount, so you're able to get the books cheaply and repackage them. Maybe you've had a slipcase created, a little cardboard cover with full-color art for your book collection to fit into. **It's a great way to sell books beyond just selling them one at a time.**

NUMBER SIX: home study courses. These may include printed products along with audio, video, or other related types of information. **A home study course is usually a bigger**

package of information than, say, a manual, book, or an audio CD by itself. Maybe it's meant to be digested over a month, or three months, or even six months. Or maybe, if it's educational—like a college course, for example—it's delivered over a semester or an entire school year. **It's information that people go through in a systematic nature, so you're teaching or revealing things in a certain order.** By the time they're finished with that course, they have a complete education on whatever it is that you're promoting, or whatever it is you're trying to convey to them.

NUMBER SEVEN: tests and quizzes. These could be self-scoring or computer scoring. I would think that if you're publishing information products, you'll want something automated. There's actually software available that can administer your test or quiz. **You can create websites that develop material for the entire course, so there would be audio and video and text on a website, and then a quiz would be there too, so people would pay to go through the course material and to take the quiz.** It's all administered online, at their own pace—and when they're done, they pass or they fail. Maybe they can print out a certificate that says "You've completed this course in XYZ." Assuming they don't need official accreditation, you can make them a master of whatever it is that they've just studied. **People will pay for your tests and quizzes because they want the education, and want to be able to have that certificate that says they've completed the course, or whatever it is.**

NUMBER EIGHT: seminar or speech transcripts. This would be combining two kinds of information products, because if you have a seminar or a speech, it was audio in the

beginning; but then you've taken that and turned it into printed transcripts. So let's say you had an event where you revealed highly-specialized, very valuable information to your attendees over the course of, say, eight hours. Let's say that by the time they paid for the event fee and all the travel expenses, it cost them each a total of $5,000 to attend.

Obviously, that information is very valuable indeed... so what would people who *didn't* attend the live event pay to receive it after the fact, in another form? What you do then is you take those eight hours of information, which you also recorded in audio format, and turn it into print form. The transcript itself becomes valuable, because other people paid $5,000 to get the same exact information in the original format. Let's say that you offer that transcript to people for $500. So for 10% of the original cost to come and attend the live event, they can just get the transcript. That's an extreme example, but **you can offer a printed transcript of just about anything you did live, whether it was a speech you gave or a seminar people attended, and make a nice additional profit.**

NUMBER NINE: newsletters. Again, as with books, newsletters are self-explanatory. You know what a newsletter is. **It involves selling your information on a subscription basis, usually; either your customers pay by the month or by the year, and you regularly deliver a printed newsletter to them.** Now, a lot of newsletters have gone online these days; and I think that's usually because people are being cheap. They want to have an easy way to deliver the content, so they've moved online what used to be done in print. And I think maybe there are some mistakes being made in the information publishing world by people trying to do it on the cheap, because there's still a lot of value in a printed and mailed newsletter. **So as you think about information products, consider the printed newsletter format rather than the digital option.** I think the old way builds more value, because you're actually delivering something to people that they can open in the mail and read cover to cover like they would read a newspaper or a magazine. These types of newsletters are definitely a valuable part of the information marketing world.

NUMBER 10: back issues of newsletters or reports. Again, if you already have a newsletter, **one of the ways you can make more money with that same information is to package up your back issues.** Maybe you have a portfolio of them that you can offer to new subscribers for free, as an incentive to subscribe. Many people would jump at the chance to get an extra 12 months for free, for example. So even though you're giving it away for free, you can make more money as more people subscribe.

NUMBER 11: other continuity products, where you can charge people a monthly fee to deliver content every month. For example: a Book of the Month club, where you're delivering a new and different book every month. You can also add something extra associated with your field. Let's say you're in the marketing field, so you select and deliver a new marketing book monthly. Every member gets a copy of that book, but then they also get your commentary on the book, where you draw attention to pages they might really want to pay attention to. **You're charging your clients not just for that book, but for the additional content that enriches what you've given them.**

NUMBER 12: a set of cards. These might be reminder cards, or recipe cards. This is an interesting concept; not having tried it myself, I'm not sure how much value there is in it, but it's one of products listed here, so do consider it. Basically, you package up cards and deliver them to people.

NUMBER 13: forms. You can offer information on time management systems, step-by-step processes, and any other kinds of forms that people would find valuable. We once had a book of fax forms, full of cover pages for various things that you might want to fax. **Someone made money by putting together this book full of forms, and you could do the same with, say, legal forms.** Quasi-legal forms that help out people in the legal realm, so that they don't have to deal with an attorney, can be very handy.

NUMBER 14: posters. You can create posters of all kinds of things, just very cool posters that people would want to have on their walls. There are poster websites that sell all kinds of posters that you could get ideas from. They could be posters for a specific purpose, or just posters that look nice.

NUMBER 15—the final item for this paper-and-ink chapter—is multi-author publications, where several authors contribute to one product and each gets to sell it. We have done many information products where experts have come together and contributed their own content, and then all of us got the rights to sell and promote that product. In a lot of cases, those products have been audio, and I'll discuss that in more detail in later chapters; but it can be done with books as well. **There are a lot of books out there where a bunch of different authors each took a chapter and developed it.** Maybe you take 10 authors, and each author writes just 20 pages—and you've got a 200-page book. **Everybody contributes a little to the project and in the end, you've got a very valuable**

product that can be sold for a significant price. Everybody gets the rights to sell it, and you've got joint ownership to a valuable product.

Perception is Reality

Now, having outlined these 15 basic types of printed information products, I hope you understand that in large part, **what really matters is how you package your information. Perception really is reality; and in the information marketing world, it's a reality that can make you a lot of money.** For instance, you can use the same basic information in a number of products. I've got a hardback book that I sell on Amazon.com called *How to Make Millions Sitting on Your Ass*. That's really the title! It's a beautiful hardback book over 600 pages long, and it sells for $29. It's all about how to make millions of dollars doing copywriting and working on the marketing of your business, and all of the other work you do when you're sitting on your ass, thinking deeply about working *on* your business, not *in* your business.

That book could easily be repackaged to sell for a couple of hundred dollars. You could put the same material in a three-ring binder, so that it looks more like something that was created just for them. It doesn't look like it's mass-produced, even though it may be. **And let me re-emphasize that it could be the *same exact* material, with absolutely no changes except that it was typeset or laid out slightly differently for the new format. Think about that.** The book that sells for $29 could easily sell for $300 or $400, because perception is reality. **You simply change the perception of the material by the way you package it.** And that's fine, since what people are buying is the results. **They're buying the perceived value of the information, not the packaging.**

Often, we writers want books because it makes us feel good to have one. It's good for our egos. I'm telling on myself here, because I've got about 25 or 30 of them right now. When you can hand somebody a book and it's got your name and photo on it, you feel great! **And books do serve their purpose; they're an excellent part of any diverse information product mix. But I want you to understand that by repackaging this material in different ways, you can dramatically increase the value of it.** We learned that firsthand. When we first got started, we considered ourselves to be in the self publishing business; but all that shifted in the early 1990s, when we started looking at all these different ways to package and sell information. We now consider ourselves to be in the information marketing business. **We quickly learned that by altering the way you package your information, you can create all kinds of new products.**

It really is only limited by your imagination. For example, we write a lot of long form sales letters. We call them special reports, because calling them special reports sounds more official, more valuable, and more important. When somebody sends away for a special report, from a marketing standpoint, you don't necessarily want people to send away for a simple sales letter. You want to say, "Send for my portfolio," or "Send for my special report," or "Send for my discovery package."

What's in a name anyway? We've never done tips sheets, but we've done lots of comparison charts. A comparison chart is usually just on one page, and it compares our products to all the other stuff that's out there. Number eight on my list was seminar transcripts, and this list of 40 information products doesn't cover seminars specifically. **Yet seminars are an awesome information product—just incredibly awesome.** Some of our seminars have sold for as much as $5,000 and $6,000. We know somebody who sells weekend seminars for $25,000. The stack of physical materials you have when that gentleman sends you home is very, very thin. Basically, you're just going there to get the information he provides.

The first time we did a seminar was September 22, 1990. **I'll never forget that day if I live to be 100, because that day that changed my life.** I mean it. It's in the top 10 most important things that have ever happened to me personally. Our joint venture partner, Russ von Hoelscher, helped us get through that first seminar. It was very frightening! Now, if you're a typical writer, you're probably an introverted person. You're comfortable spending long hours by yourself behind a computer, month after month, year after year; so your social skills tend to get a little rusty. Maybe you even become mildly socially retarded. The idea of getting up in front of a group of people and performing publicly might just scare you to death.

If it does, let me assure you that I've never spoken to anyone who has ever confessed to me that they were more scared than I was on September 22, 1990. And you know what? I was scared to death for the first ten years we did seminars; right up until about the year 2000. During that period we did dozens of them; and by now (mid-2011), we've done nearly 300 seminars total. It's easier now, but the first 10 years were simply frightening. **Yet I wanted to do seminars so badly because, as information products, they just rock.** They're scary; but of course, oftentimes, what's the most scary is also the most exciting. My best analogy there is the rollercoaster. Some roller coasters are so intense that people pass out. They're very, very frightening and yet they're very exciting as well... and perhaps that excitement is part and parcel of the fright.

So although they're not *specifically* mentioned in the 40, **I want you to consider seminars, workshops, and roundtable events, which is where you bring in a small group of your customers and sell to them directly.** By the way, that's really how we cut our teeth on seminars. Our first seminar, the one we did with Russ, attracted about 140 people in Wichita, Kansas, so it was pretty big. But the next 13-15 seminars we did were all tiny events that we handled ourselves. It was just my wife Eileen, a couple of our staff members, and myself. We brought in small groups of our customers, 10-12 people at a time. **As you conduct more seminars, large or small, your confidence will increase—and so will the range of products you have to offer.** Just in the last 10 years, Chris Lakey and I have developed a large number of information products from the content we produced during seminars.

Newsletters, which we've been publishing for years, are also incredibly versatile. **The thing I like about newsletters is that the material in our newsletters also ends up in our books and some of our other home study courses**—and the few customers who realize this don't even care. **We often republish the same information in a variety of ways a number of times, in order to reach the maximum number of individual customers.** The overlap is minor, and again, the customers who realize that you've used something from your newsletter in your home study course or book don't mind. They understand that you're trying to leverage your information (and you do have tremendous leverage here), so they're not going to be upset. If they are, you could just comp them something—that is, give them something free.

You can keep these people happy; they're the kind of people who are *easy* to keep happy, actually, because they're the serious students. **Typically, the customers who cause you the most problems are those who buy the least from you...** and those are the ones who are easiest to get rid of anyway, because they don't do that much business with you. Customers who buy everything that you do end up causing you fewer problems.

I hope you can see how that all of this really does tie together. And remember: when you're doing any live event, such as a seminar, teleseminar, or workshop, be sure that you're recording. **You can convert those events to audio and printed products both. Ultimately, any audio product can become a print product.** This printed product began as an audio product that we later had transcribed. The transcripts went to our ghostwriter, Floyd Largent, who turned them into newsletters and a book. That's how we do things. That's how we've been doing things for over two decades now.

By the way, **there are dirt-cheap transcription services on the Internet. Ditto for editing services.** There are plenty of ghostwriters out there who can work with your material, although finding a good ghostwriter may be very, very challenging. If you're serious about wanting to find a ghostwriter, I can give you Floyd Largent's contact information if you can't find him by Googling.

One 70-minute phone call or event that we record works out to about 25,000 words transcribed. Try writing 25,000 words; even a fast writer will take a while to write that many words. I consider myself a fast writer, when I get on a roll, and even then I can only write about 2,000 words an hour. I consider that very, very fast. But think about it: all we do is talk for 70 minutes, and that translates to more than 10 hours worth of writing. **Then you give that material to a ghostwriter, or you smooth it out yourself using your own writing skills.** Because here's the thing: just because something sounds good, and you can understand it from an audio perspective, that doesn't mean that it doesn't require a lot of clean-up at the transcription level. A lot of things are lost in the translation from audio to print, and there's often some redundancy to be trimmed away. So either you need to use your own writing skills and smooth it out, or work with a ghostwriter like Floyd Largent and let him do his magic.

I find all this to be very exciting stuff, and we've just gotten started on all the different things that you can do to make money with information marketing. **I just hope you can see the cohesiveness of the information marketing options here, that it all works together.** You really can use and reuse the same information, if you're creative about how to present it. **Don't get hung up on any of these individual options, especially books.** I know that all writers want books, because I'm speaking for myself as a writer, but that may not be the most profitable venue to choose. In fact, it usually isn't, because **the way that you make the big bucks is by repackaging your information in as many different formats as possible.** Books are mostly for our own egos; and maybe that's why, when people think about information publishing, they think about one thing. This is especially true of people who want to be considered experts on something. They think that the only way to have credibility is to have a book. That's all they can muster up the strength or the creativity to imagine.

So they sit down and open up Microsoft Word, and spend some time staring at a blank screen, thinking, "Okay. What's my book going to be about?" They try to figure out what the title of their book's going to be. Then they spend some time jotting down or typing out some rough notes. I would imagine that after a few minutes of that, the creative juices have stopped flowing. They're out of ideas. When that happens, or when it just doesn't come together like they thought it would or as *quickly* as they thought it would, they give up. **They never even entertain any other ideas, because they're focused on the idea that they *must* have a book.**

And yes, it's a good idea, no doubt: having your own book is an excellent step toward establishing your credibility as an expert in your field. However, it's not the be all-end all of credibility. It's not a requirement. It's not something you *have* to have in order to be taken seriously. **There reality is that there are easier ways to publish information than trying to have your own book.** Maybe the book comes later, tapping into information you've published in other areas. Maybe it comes from the transcription of an audio product. **Your book doesn't need to happen right away.** These other paper-and-ink products are probably a better place to get started.

I've always been fond of newsletters as information products. Now, they're not as easy to sell as some products, because you have to get people to see the value of subscribing on a monthly basis. But then again, maybe you can sell a newsletter for an annual fee; there are benefits to both approaches. I've seen newsletters offered for $49.99 for one year, or two years for $20.00 more. It's easy to do things like that. **And speaking of newsletters, right now we're on a five-year roll with two of**

ours. As the back issues stack up, they just become more valuable, to both us and our customers. When this happens, you can give the back issues away as free bonus gifts, and they can become part of your home study courses or seminar handouts. They're a valuable resource.

With newsletters, you can profit from doing just a little bit of writing every month. I think this is something that just about anybody can do, assuming that you have a computer, the ability to type, and minimal writing skills. If you wanted to publish a newsletter of four, eight, or 12 pages per month (whatever that length may be), then you just divide that length into the number of days in the month to determine how much you have to write every day. It ends up being a lot less than it would be if you were going about the daunting task of trying to produce a 300-page book. **You may end up having to write less than a half a page a day to reach your goal—allowing leeway for rewriting, editing, and packaging, of course.**

Now, you may not do it that way. Some days you may write two pages, some days one, some days nothing. Maybe when it gets down to the wire, you finish up the final half of the newsletter in a day because you procrastinated the rest of the month. All that's fine, as long as you leave yourself time for the other prep work. But the point is, if you can write as little as four pages, you can have a newsletter. Actually, I suppose you could even have a one-page newsletter. You could even position yourself that way: "This is the easiest newsletter to read, ever, because it's only one page. You don't have to sift through page after page. I'm going to keep it short, sweet, and to the point."

Maybe you could even use something like the tip sheet model, where it's one page of very specialized know-how, delivered monthly. Even at one page long, it's so valuable that it's worth whatever price you're selling it for. **You just have to determine what your content is, and match that content to a group of people who are eager to learn that content... and who are willing to pay a lot of money for it.** That's the part that we can't do for you; you have to figure out for yourself what industry that's going to be in. Are you selling to businesses, or consumers? What is your target marketplace? What are they interested in? What kind of information will they spend money on? You have to answer all those questions, and then you have to decide if that's something of interest to you. In our marketplace, the opportunity market, people are willing to spend a lot on information, tools, and resources that help them make money from home.

So for example, we could produce a one-page newsletter that shares a valuable marketing or money-making tip, and that would be something we would sell to our marketplace. You have to explore the possibilities for your own marketplace; and those possibilities are worth exploring. **Newsletters, I think, are a very good way to get started, given the relative ease of writing them over the course of a month.** That's not to say that it's always easy. Lots of people have started newsletters and never finished them. But the possibilities are wide open, and the content for newsletters can come from all kinds of places. **In fact, you could have guest writers writing content for your newsletters.** In other words, just as you can do with any of these content items, you can have someone else do all the work!

The Core Message

In the 23 years we've been in business here at M.O.R.E.,

Inc., I believe we've done all 15 of the types of information products I presented in this chapter, except tip sheets and card sets—although we had a business at one point that was related to Thank You cards, so arguably, we *have* done those kinds of products. We've even done boxed book sets, some of them digital, and we've actually dabbled in tests and quizzes, although we've never developed that fully. **Again, I think that the key here is not to get too hung up on any one specific type product.** One of the things that you'll hear me talk about on a fairly regular basis (and I know I've done it several times already in this book) is that **the marketplace comes before the product; you need to worry more about the people you're selling to than about the specific products you're selling to those people.**

If you get hung up on a product, what often happens is this: you'll be in a situation where you've got this idea for a great product and you know who you're going to sell it to, so you spend all this time developing it and then you try to market it to your marketplace—and they don't respond. You've just poured your heart into this one project, and for whatever reason, your prospects don't respond well. You're left feeling a bit jaded; you're frustrated. You may give up on your business dreams altogether.

Let's say you spend all that time and money writing a book. It's your baby, and you love it. Then you go out there and you try to sell it—and the sales are flat. People just don't respond like you thought they would. You had 5,000 of them printed so you could get the printing cheap, and now you've got a garage full of books that you can't sell, and your family and friends all laugh at you. So you just put that project aside. Maybe you even shred all those books so you never have to look at them again, or maybe they're boxed up in a storage shed somewhere and you're kind of ashamed of them. You move on with your life, having accomplished nothing.

That can happen when you're so focused on a single product that you're not looking at the big picture of serving your marketplace. But if you'll work with your marketplace first in mind, you'll know what kind of things they're interested in, and you can try to develop products that those people want. If something doesn't work, you can say, "Well, if they don't buy this, they might buy *that*, and I'm not really that concerned about what they might buy on an individual basis. If I try to introduce a newsletter to my marketplace and they don't respond, that doesn't offend me. I'm not really jaded that much by that experience. I'm a little upset, but I'm not hugely upset, and I'm not offended.

"So what I'm going to do is take that same content and make it into a book. If they don't buy a book, then I'm going to make it into a report. And if they don't buy a report, I'm going to put on a seminar. **I'm just going to refuse to give up, because I know this marketplace that I'm serving. I know what kinds of things they're interested in;** so I'm just looking for the right combination, the right format, the right information product they want to buy... and I'm not going to let one failure get in my way. I'm going to keep trying other ways to present my information to them."

In our business, we teach people how to make money, and we provide business opportunities. Some of our clients respond really well to one kind of information product, and others respond to other kinds of information products. **But we**

don't get too hung up on presenting the information in a certain way. We have a message that we want to share with people in different formats, and it's the same basic message, even though in some cases it might be presented on audio and in others it might be presented in book format. In still other cases, that material might be presented through a newsletter, or a home study course, or a report. **Our core message stays the same, even though the type of paper-and-ink that we use to distribute that information to clients may change.**

When you think about a guru in any field, what they teach is the same all the time, really. They've got a method for how they share their information; how they do that might change from time to time or from market to market, but their core information stays the same, and the things that they teach are all based on their experiences. **So you're going to get the same message every time you hear them give a presentation.** If you buy their book, you're going to find out that the book conveys the same message you've already heard them present on audio.

So do what they do: stay focused on serving your marketplace first, and then all of these kinds of information products—the paper-and-inks, the audios, and all the others that arise from them—will just be different ways that you're trying to present your message to your marketplace. *Focus on the marketplace first.* Don't get too hung up on any of these specific kinds of products, because if you pour your heart and soul into one specific area or format and it doesn't get the response you're looking for, it can leave you with a bad taste in your mouth. **Whereas if you know your message is strong and you know your marketplace is strong, all you've got to do is figure out the right method and medium to reach them with.** Let the way you deliver your information change as you try to serve that marketplace, presenting different options for delivering the main information that you want to share with them.

It's all about developing relationships with customers, and reselling them as many different things as possible for as much profit as possible as often as possible, for the largest possible amount of money per transaction. That's essentially what business is. The info marketers who make the most money are the ones who do what every good business in the world does: they try to develop customers and resell them again and again.

And remember, customers for information products tend to be insatiable. One of my favorite stories on this topic involves one of our company's Vice Presidents, Randy Hamilton. He's a very smart guy, a Mensa member—and you have to have an IQ at the top of the scale to qualify for that. Well, when he first started working with us back in the early 1990s, we had five or six different publications that we were selling. We were still just getting started, you see. I've already told you about our little manual called *Dialing for Dollars* and the distributorships we sold through that product, which allowed our clients to sell four or five other little manuals on their own.

Randy looked at our product line and was not impressed with it at all. Frankly, it wasn't much to look at. I find our original product line to be kind of embarrassing to review these days. It was just so poorly written. Now, I don't consider myself a great writer now, but 20 years ago I was just terrible. Well, Randy told himself, "Man, I've got to get my resume out there. This company is going under within a year. There's no way this company is going to make it!" Then he went back to work—and we had plenty of work. The orders were coming in like crazy.

Then, every month or so, he'd say, "Man, I got to get my resume out there, because this company is *not* going to last." Now, Randy's a smart guy. He understands business in general... but he didn't understand the information business. Not then. This went on for three or four years. Every month at first, then every six months, and then every eight months, and then every ten months, and then once a year he'd think, "Man, this company just won't last." But here we are; we're still going strong.

That's because some people have an insatiable demand for the products we offer. **People who buy information products just can't seem to get enough of them.** Randy didn't understand that then, and that's no fault of his. Most people don't get it, and never understand it. But we have customers who've been with us for 5, 10, or 15 years. Some people (admittedly very few), have been with us now for a couple of decades—basically since shortly after we opened our doors. These folks just keep rebuying and rebuying, so we keep reselling and reselling.

That's how you build business success: you resell to the same customers repeatedly, the same way that a successful restaurant or any other business does. If you've got a retail store, you want to get the same people to come back again and again. So you keep coming up with more and different products to sell. When many people get started, they have no idea how they're going to accomplish this; they're just aghast at all the possibilities. They ask themselves, "My God. How am I going to do that?" Well, here it is. Here's how you're going to create a ton of information products of all different kinds.

You begin at the beginning. You have an initial product that you sell, like we had our little manual, *Dialing for Dollars*.

We sold 160,000 of those manuals in five years, so we had 160,000 customers. Then we brought in Russ von Hoelscher, and he helped us develop special offers to resell to those people. Because here's the thing: **when somebody buys from you once, the ice is broken and the relationship starts. This is a business that's very dependent on relationships.** People want to know who they're buying from, so we need to get to know them. If you had a small restaurant, for example, you'd want to go around and shake your customers' hands, even get to know them on a first-name basis.

Now, I realize that for a writer, this can be difficult; because again, writers tend to be introverts. But the information that you write and sell goes a long way towards establishing and building those relationships. **Even if you never meet customers in person, you can get personal with them in print.** When we start talking about audio, that becomes really important, because by hearing your voice people can get a sense of who you are. Ditto for when they purchase your video products, or come to your workshops and get to meet you face-to-face. For some of us, the personal interaction is difficult at first; but over time, it becomes easier.

And here's the bottom line. Once you have a customer base, if you're not trying to go back and resell them something, then you're losing money—and nobody in their right mind wants to lose money. **So you need to sit down and develop other information products that are similar and somehow related to what you sold them the first time.** As I said, **it's only limited by your imagination...** and really, this list of 40 is incomplete. I've already told you there are two types of information products that aren't even on this list: one is seminars and workshops, and the other is coaching and consulting programs. Here's another one: websites. I consider a website to be an invaluable information product, and we've developed and sold a ton of them over the years.

So never stop thinking about the relationship-building aspect of this business. And remember, the way you package your information is all based on perception. If you're producing information products that really try to help people do something, then the more they pay, the more they pay *attention*. **It's a simple fact: the more money somebody pays for something, the more seriously they take it.** It's as true for information as it is for anything else in the world.

There's a marketing consultant whom I've personally paid over a hundred grand to over the years; I will not identify him by name. Now, I have a good friend who knows about this. He's watched me do business with this guy for a number of years, and he's seen all the money I've paid to participate in this consultant's coaching programs, to go to his seminars, and to be part of his inner circle that meets a few times a year. I've shelled out big bucks to get the information this guy is selling.

And this friend who knows that I've spent this fortune says, "Hey, TJ, you're getting ripped off, because the same information you're paying thousands of dollars for you can get at the bookstore. This guy's got about a dozen books for sale. For a couple hundred dollars, you can buy every book he's ever published, and you can get all that same information." My friend has a point, but what he doesn't realize is that this is not exactly true. I've got thousands of books. I've got so many books that I throw or give hundreds of them away every year, and I just keep buying more. I have many books that I've never read from cover to cover. I skim them, but I buy them faster than I can read them, and I'm afraid I just don't take books that seriously.

But when I go to a seminar, where I'm held captive and I've got to shut my cell phone off and just there and listen, I take a million notes. When I've gone to some of these inner circle meetings where there's a small group of people and you've got to sit in a room for two or three days with that little group, man, **I take that seriously. So I'm absorbing all this information in my own way.** And yes, my friend is right. I could in fact have bought all of this guy's books for less than $200, and gotten all the same information he teaches at his seminars and inner circle meetings. **But it wouldn't have had the same impact on me.** The truth is, this consultant has helped me a tremendous amount. It's because I paid this huge sum of money that I've been able to absorb all his best teachings.

Again, the important thing here is not to get too focused on the details of a particular kind of information product. The tendency, I think, is to always go specific. "I need to write a book. I'm going to create a newsletter." To a large degree, that gets you focused on the wrong things. **The more you're able to maintain focus on the customers you're serving,** *not* **the specific products you offer them, the better you'll do.** If you can remain focused on customers first, you'll have the ability to develop a never-ending stream of information products that they'll be interested in buying.

Of course, you do have to focus on the product when you're creating it. If you want to write a book, you've got to sit down and write, or otherwise come up with the content. Maybe you're using transcribed audio as a shortcut of sorts. If you're doing a newsletter, obviously at some point you have to write or find the content for it. Time needs to be set aside for that, but I think in the early stages, it's *much* more important to focus on your marketplace. Find the group of people you're going to serve, and then spend a lot of time thinking about what they want the most. Next, work to develop a line of information products in an attempt to give them exactly that. **That's what it's all about: serving the marketplace in as many ways as possible. That will manifest itself, in some cases, as books; in other cases, it'll be newsletters, home study courses, and the other kinds of products that we're talking about here.**

If you start out by worrying about one kind of product, and thus narrowing your focus from the very beginning, I think you're missing the larger message here of serving your marketplace, and then through that, developing paper-and-ink information products that those people want to buy. **I recommend that you go back and review the section earlier in this chapter regarding the 15 types of paper-and-ink information products that you can easily create.** Read over them, highlight passages, underline things, and even take notes. **Then think about the types of information products that you could create within each category.**

What kind of reports could you write? What kind of tip sheets could you write? What kind of manuals could you write? What kind of books could you write? What boxed sets could you create? If you're going to do a home study course, what would that look like? What kind of tests and quizzes could you create? Seminars, newsletters, back issues of newsletters, continuity items, cards, forms, posters, and multi-author publications; you've got options with all of those. **Some may work better than others when you're just starting out, but the point is** that you have to seriously consider each type. So please, don't focus on any particular one individually until you start thinking more about your marketplace first.

Have some fun thinking about all the ways you can create and develop paper-and-ink information products, but don't ever lose sight of the marketplace. **Focus on your customers, and the products will come as you try to serve that marketplace, and as you find ways to deliver your main message to them. Be creative.** I promised you at the beginning of this chapter (and elsewhere in this book) that this is a very creative way to make money. And that's a wonderful thing. Part of the reason why most people are attracted to writing in the first place is because of the artistic nature of it.

Imagination and creativity are first cousins here, and this form of information marketing is extremely creative. It's not business in a way that you would normally think of business. This is fun; it's exciting. Furthermore, it's deeply rewarding and fulfilling to take a product, or a series of products, or an endless number of products that you've created yourself, and make money on them without depending on some publisher to sell them for you. **You're taking charge of your own life,** damn it. **This is a tremendous way to profit. It can be so artistic because it transcends writing; but it's still taking stuff that came from you and from your imagination, your creativity, and turning it into tremendous amounts of money.**

CHAPTER TEN:

Audio/Video Options

Last chapter, I talked about printed products; **in this chapter, I'll cover audio and video.** Let me just say this: A lot of people whom I can imagine buying this book—a lot of writers—probably don't see themselves as people who have the ability to communicate in any way other than writing. If that's how you feel, I can't blame you a bit. You might think, for example, that for someone to produce a decent audio product, they'd have to be a good public speaker. But that's not necessarily so. **What people are really looking for is the valuable information you present, not how you present it.**

In the information marketing business, people want results. They want experts. **They want somebody to tell them exactly what to do, somebody to lead them in the right direction.** As a general rule, when you're writing and producing written information products, you're taking the position of the expert. **You're helping people get what they really want, which is total certainty. They're looking for results.** They want to know exactly what to do, and they tend to admire people that have strong attitudes one way or another. Not wishy-washy people, but people who tell them exactly how it is, and how it should be, and what they should do.

You're already offering this, if you're committed to getting paid to write and you're using information marketing to get ahead—and you'd be crazy not to, as far as I'm concerned, because **this *is* such a lucrative business option.** Here we are, just a little, tiny company in the middle of Kansas. If you didn't know we were an hour north of Wichita, you'd never be able to find Goessel on a map. We're just a drop in the bucket, a small collection of 400 people out in the middle of nowhere. And yet, starting with only a few hundred dollars, M.O.R.E., Inc. has been able to amass over $140 million in total sales in 23 years. **That's *all* because of information marketing, and the fact that we're practicing what we preach.**

We made a commitment to learn how to master the art of copywriting, which was the first topic I covered in this book. We've used ghostwriters extensively, which was the second aspect of this program. And we've been deeply committed to trying to become the best we can possibly be in this area of information marketing. Here's where it all comes together, folks.

For those of you who just consider yourselves to be writers and feel that you have no ability to get out and perform in front of a live audience as a speaker, or to produce audio/video programs, realize first of all that somebody could always just read your writing for you. **You don't have to be the one who actually records your ideas.** If there's just no way on God's green Earth that I'm ever going to convince you that you're quite capable of producing audio, and that you *should* do it, you can always hire somebody else to take your written materials and deliver them in the audio format.

But relax: you *can* do audio, at least. The truth is, some of the people who are making the most money with audio programs aren't very good communicators at all. They stutter; they're not professional in any way. **Chris Lakey and I**

certainly don't consider ourselves to be professional speakers. But whatever we lack in professionalism, we try to make up for by being totally real, totally authentic, totally raw, and very enthusiastic about what we teach. So I don't consider myself to be a public speaker, but **I learned early on that whenever I write about a subject, the more that I *do* write about it, the more strongly I can communicate it in other media.** So there's a connection between writing and then speaking about the subjects you write about. **The more you focus on writing about specific topics, the easier it will be for you to do audio and video.**

Why Consider Audio/Video At All?

Here are five reasons why you should consider creating audio and video products; and remember, **the *why* is more important than the *how*.** Later in the chapter, we're going to go into specific detail on 10 different kinds of audio/video programs that you can do, as well as some offshoots of those 10. But let's look at these reasons why you should do them first; and **the FIRST reason is, it's just so easy!** By and large, an audio or video product is the easiest kind of information product that you can produce, especially a purely audio product. It *does* help if you like talking. Me, I've always been the kind of person that can't keep my mouth shut. Ever since I was just a little kid, I've just been a talker.

Now, I've had some really expensive recording equipment over the years; we've been producing audio now for over 20 years. But our very first audio product was on cassette tape. Remember those? The *Dialing for Dollars* booklet came with a little cassette tape, all for $12.95. We did that tape on an inexpensive recorder. Now, of course, that was back in the 1980s; we haven't produced cassette tapes for years. **It's all audio CD and MP3s, where you can cram many, many hours onto one thin disc of plastic and metal or even deliver it online, so your costs are next to nothing.**

After we got more sophisticated, we used to go into a studio and pay $30-40 an hour to produce our audio. A few years later I had this technical wizard in Newton, Kansas, come into the company, and I spent about $10,000 on this fancy set-up he created. It would do everything; it had all the bells and whistles and dials. It was an elaborate piece of machinery, and we recorded on it for about 10 years. But it was way more than I needed. **I recorded the audio product that this book was based on using a $50 audio recorder from Radio Shack. I ran it through a little phone patch that you can buy for $100 or less that makes it easy to record phone calls.** So the equipment cost here is next to nothing, and it's really easy to use.

The SECOND reason you should embrace audio products is that they're very valuable to certain people. A lot of our customers just love audio. **I understand that, because I'm addicted to audio myself.** I can't jump in my car and drive anywhere unless I've got something to listen to... and I get really tired of listening to music, so I'm always listening to some audio program or other. In fact, I just spent $397 this morning buying some CDs from a speaker that I've been listening to. I've really been enjoying listening to this guy... and you can buy all his audio products for $397. Hell of a deal! While I was driving down the road listening to him, I heard his phone number on his audio program, so I simply called the number. His father answered the phone (his father works for him) and took my credit card order.

I've spent thousands and thousands of dollars on audio programs. My car is actually a learning machine; it's also my office. I'm always talking on the phone. I'm always writing, taking notes, reading, and doing similar things while I'm driving. I can't go anywhere without listening to audio. A lot of our customers are the same way. People just love audio. It's easy to produce, and has a high perceived value. That's an ideal combination for an informational product!

The Number THREE reason to create audio products: it's fast, especially if you specialize. Chris and I are very familiar with information marketing; we've been doing it for 23 years. We don't even have to compile extensive notes in advance to be able to speak with real authority on the subject. **So basically, once you're working within a certain niche market and consistently producing information that's centered around that market, and you know your stuff, it's very, very simple to create a new audio product.** Now, it's not necessarily that simple to produce video; and personally, I don't like the camera. Whenever the camera's on me, I get very nervous.

But producing audio is just so easy! **We do seminars every month, and we create audio whenever we do the seminars.** This little system I have down here in the basement of my house lets me record audio very easily. It's fast—and as you know, time is money. Chris and I are getting ready to start on a new project right after we finish this one, and we expect that we're going to be working on this new project for as much as a year. We'll do just a little bit every week, and at the end of the year, we'll have a huge catalog filled with all these individual products we can sell. It's just so fast, so easy, so simple!

Now for the FOURTH reason you should do audio products: audio can easily be transcribed and then repackaged. We've actually sold or given away as bonuses some of our audio transcripts. They add value to the package. In the previous chapter, I talked about home study courses and that type of thing, where you give people multimedia packages. **You want to give them CDs, DVDs, and transcripts, so that when they open the box, it's like Christmas when they were a kid.** There are all these different pieces inside. People like that. When they spend hundreds of dollars on an information product, they like opening the box and seeing all these different things.

You can just have the audio transcribed, or you can also do what we do. The transcripts for our entire *Get Paid to Write* audio program went to our ghostwriter, Floyd Largent in San Antonio, Texas. Floyd edited it into a format that we used for this book, and also for some newsletters. We may convert it into other printed formats later, because **we recycle this material as many ways as we can. And again, it's just so easy and simple for us now.** It used to be difficult to find people to supply those kinds of services, but not anymore: you can find them for reasonable rates on the Internet. **Now we just send the audio to transcribers and the resulting transcriptions to Floyd, and he creates all kinds of written products out of our audio programs.**

Number FIVE is the icing on the cake; I saved the very best for last. **To me there is no faster, simpler, and easier way to build relationships with large groups of people than by creating audio products.** There's just something about audio that makes it a real relationship builder. We meet people all the time at our seminars, and they tell us over and over again, "Oh, man, I feel like I know you." If I had $1,000 for every time I've had a client say that to me, I'd be a billionaire! Why do they feel like they know me? Some of it is the writing that we do for them, but it's mostly the audio. **A talented writer can get inside people's hearts and heads and do that all-important relationship building, but audio is even more direct.**

You see, prospects are always asking themselves, "Can I trust this person?" Often this is rather unconscious, sometimes very unconscious; but some people are like me, aware of it all the time. They're always wondering about it at some level. **If you're sending written stuff, you can do things that satisfy that desire to trust;** you can tell them about yourself, tell them some personal stories (maybe funny ones), and get very personable with them. A talented writer has the skills to do that... but they can also mask things. A highly skilled but dishonest writer could probably make people trust them just because they were a highly skilled writer. And admittedly, the same thing goes for a really slick, professional speaker. Con men do it all the time: they gain people's confidence because they fool people.

But for the most part, we don't fool people in audio presentations, since most of us can't fool people at all. They'll listen to you on the audio to gauge the type of person you are, and many times the people who are really serious buyers, repeat buyers, will listen to you again and again. I've done it. I have audio programs that I've listened to—and I'm not exaggerating—well over a hundred times, to the point where the speaker is inside my head. I've got an audio program that I've listened to since 1983 or 1984, and the guy's voice is still in my head. Even though I never met him personally and he's been dead for years now, his voice is still ringing in my head. **The**

things that he said on that audio changed my life, helped motivate me to set my standards higher, helped me set higher goals, helped me to want to push myself harder and try to do more with my life when I was in my early 20s.

When I talk about relationship-building, that's really what I'm talking about: your ability to influence people, your ability to make people trust you. In a good business relationship, your customers feel like they know you, that they can trust you; they feel affinity with you at some level. Naturally, people want to do business with people that they know and trust. If they listen to you on the audio, they'll get a sense of who you are and that they can trust you and like you, all of which is crucial when it comes to trying to resell them again and again—which is how all businesses make money.

Audio is a great way to warm people up to you, so you definitely need to add audio products into your product mix. We can attest to its value for effectively imparting information. We've recorded, produced, and published thousands of audio programs, on a wide variety of subjects in our field, ranging from general marketing strategies to more specific types of advice. For example, we've published audio products on making money in real estate. We've published audio products on making money on eBay. We've published audio programs on copywriting and marketing, and things like this product. Remember, *Get Paid to Write* was an audio product first. We have a library jam-packed full of our official audio products.

But beyond that, we also use audio for selling. We've delivered special reports on audio; in fact, in the past we've actually read our sales letters directly into audio. We've also produced audio information products to go along with offers

to do business with us. There's a reason we do all that: **it's effective.** I've already told you some of the reasons, but what it comes down to is this: **in many cases, the spoken word is perceived to be of much higher value than the written word.** I find that kind of funny, because it's much easier to speak than to write. As I mentioned earlier, we've learned that a 70-minute audio session (about the length of a CD) works out to about 25,000 words. Now, I just heard someone interviewed the other day on the radio, and he was talking about his new book—and how his book was about 70,000 words. That's less than three times the length of the average audio session we produce, or about 210 minutes—three and one-half hours—worth of audio. That's all it takes to fill a good-sized book.

This book happened to be sports book. I'm sure this gentleman wrote those words from scratch—and **I can guarantee that he had a lot harder time writing those 70,000 words than we do speaking 70,000 words that we might turn into print eventually.** Even with the transcription and editing, it's easier in the long run. I know that for a fact, because I've published books before that I've written from scratch. Frankly, it can be a very tedious, time-consuming, complicated thing; whereas I have no problem with recording three hours of audio.

It's especially easy when it's on some subject we're already familiar with or expert on. I can pick up the phone and call Chris Lakey, tell him we need to do this, and we can be recording in five minutes. We might jot down some quick notes for what we want to say, make sure we get our bases covered, and an hour later, we're off the phone and we've got an audio product. **If we were to sit down and decide to produce a 25,000-word printed report, it would take several weeks of**

writing, editing, and production, minimum, just to get it where we want it to be.

So you can see how easy it is to produce audio; and video is very similar these days. It used to be that video production was really complicated and took a lot of work, even after the computer revolution. You had to record first; and then, if you were going to edit on the computer, you had to convert it into a digital file. You almost had to have a degree from some fancy, expensive video editing school to do a decent job of video production and eventually spit out a DVD of some kind.

Today, video still has its issues, but it's much easier than before. Even many smartphones will record high definition video these days. Within a matter of minutes, you can have a video clip in your computer. **You can edit it fairly easily, and it takes no special skills, apparently;** that's more Chris Lakey's venue than mine! **But the point is that with a minimum of effort, you can have a video up on a website making sales for you, or providing information to clients.**

We still prefer to do audio, though, because it's so easy. In fact, when we do live events, we much prefer audio recordings to video. If you get out a video camera, the event turns into a different animal, suddenly. They have the spotlight on you, the camera's pointing right at you, and you have to perform. That makes it more complicated, at least from a personal standpoint; though otherwise, it's still easy to use. We have a friend who does a lot of video; in fact, his entire information product line is delivered via video. It's a great series, and very valuable. **Video does have a certain value above even audio; so if you can do video, realize that it can help you make even more money, helping you to reach your**

customers in a different way.

Before I move on, **let's take a quick look at how video can also help you build relationships.** As I've mentioned before, Chris Lakey is a political junkie; he enjoys reading about politics, and peruses the web all the time looking for articles to read. But what he likes even better is listening to an audio program or watching a video about politics. So if he happens to read a blog or news story and there's a video link or audio file associated with it, he'll grab that and listen to it or watch it — **because it's so much better to hear them than to read them.** For example, Chris tells me that there's a gentleman who is a historian and a political junkie like him; he's written several books and has a lot to say. Chris enjoys all the articles he writes, and he writes fairly often.

But anytime Chris sees that this guy has a new video, he watches it right away, because it helps Chris get to know the guy better. **It's a more personal relationship. I mean "relationship" in a loose sense of the word here,** but it does convey that Chris is a follower of the information that this gentlemen publishes. Chris enjoys watching and hearing him, because he gets to know more about what this man stands for, and what he's all about. **I think this is a good example of how audio and video can help with relationship building, which as you know is an important part of marketing.**

Before I go into detail about how you can do that, you need to understand the reasons why you need to do it; that's the foundation behind all your audio efforts. I hope the preceding information can help, because if you can grasp the big picture of why you need to add audio and video, **then the how and the specific ways you do it will come to you.** I think that you'll use a lot of these methods once you've gotten the passion, and once you've seen why it's valuable—just as you will with the paper-and ink-stuff that I talked about in the last chapter. Once you know it's out there, once you see what other people are doing, I think you'll soon come up with some pretty good, original methods on your own, beyond what I've got to show you here.

The more convinced you are that this is a great way for you to make money, and that it's something you should be doing, the easier it's going to be to get over those initial hurdles. Call it the comfort zone, if you want: everything is uncomfortable until it becomes comfortable. **The first that you do is going to be tough, and you may have to do a bunch of them before you're comfortable with the process.** If you're like me, you have to do a bunch of *anything* before it becomes either second nature or fun. But the more you want to do it, and the more you're convinced that it's something you *should* be doing, the easier it's going to be.

The Options

In the last chapter, I pointed out that I had a list of 40 different types of information products that you can create and sell. Of course, I actually added some that weren't on the initial list, so it's over 40 now. **In this chapter, we've got ten more, all audio/video programs, that you can consider.** Now, again, I want to you remember to back away from the concept that you need to be perfect and professional and have a radio announcer-type voice to create these products and sell them like hotcakes. That's simply not true. People will listen to information because of its value, not necessarily because they feel like you're entertaining them. As the book I got these items from points out, **"The info business does not require talent; just an understanding of your market and a little work."**

If you've got a good understanding of your marketplace, it doesn't require a special talent to produce audio or video. You don't have to have a golden voice. You don't have to be good looking. **You just have to be able to communicate, and that'll come with practice.** I know this from personal experience. Recently, someone mentioned to Chris they had seen him speak on several occasions live before an audience, and they remembered how nervous he was the first times he spoke; but they also see that today, speaking publically is like second nature to him. Put him in front of a group with something to say, and he doesn't have a problem at all. The same is true with me.

The comfort with producing audio or video will indeed come over time. Now, as I mentioned earlier, I'm still not very comfortable on DVD or video. But audio is no issue at all—and video will come. We're producing more and more videos with our business, so I do think that over time, I'll become more comfortable with it.

It doesn't require talent. **You don't have to be an expert or special at all.** But you *do* need to understand your marketplace, and you'll have to do a little work to produce the product. **With that said, here are the next 10 points, all about audio and video.**

Let's pick up with NUMBER 16, continuing from last chapter's list: **audio tape or audio CD of recorded live speeches, seminars, or consultations; anything done live.** I'm assuming here that we're talking about events conducted in front of a studio audience, in front of real people, that you recorded as you conducted them.

NUMBER 17 is audio how-to instructionals, which are usually studio-recorded. Chris just recorded a how-to instructional video, showing people how some websites that we gave them worked, and just walking them through those sites. That happened to be a video, but it could also be done on audio.

NUMBER 18 is interviews, conversations, and round-table discussions. I've spoken at length about the first audio program we did with Russ von Hoelscher way back in the early days, where we recorded a long conversation that Russ, my wife Eileen, and I had. We used to pay Russ $2,500 to have him come spend the weekend and share some strategies, to talk business, and to help us improve our business so we could do even better than we already were. **So on one trip, we stuck a tape player on the table and started asking him questions.** The final product had lot of background noise, as you can imagine: coffee cups clinking, rustled papers, and other incidental sounds. **But it contained valuable information that people wanted to learn, and they were willing to pay a reasonable price to get it.** We charged $195 for the best parts of the recordings, and they were happy to pay that instead of the $2,500 that Russ would have charged them!

NUMBER 19: a collection of radio broadcasts. This one might take a little more creativity, if you don't have a radio studio and aren't on the air already. But if you are, you could take a collection of existing broadcasts, package them together, and make them into an audio program of some kind. **If you're not a broadcaster, perhaps you could work out a joint**

venture with somebody who is; you could take the audio of
them or their radio personality, and turn it into a package of
information products. You could become the publisher,
working out an agreement where they would license you the
rights to convert their audio to a sellable information product.

Something like that could serve an excellent purpose for
your clients, depending on who it was and what the content
was. You may find that the creator has never even thought about
creating an information product. So you come to them as a
marketer and say, "Hey, you're already talking on the air for an
hour a day, and I would just like to use some of that. I'd like to
create an audio compilation of the subjects that you talk about
everyday on the radio, something that I think my clients would
be interested in buying. Let's do that and split the profits." So
think about the creative ways you could do that.

NUMBER 20: an interactive workbook. In this case,
we're kind of going back to an option we talked about in the
paper-and-ink chapter, the home study course. You could
produce a combination of print and audio here, where the
audio takes people through the workbook or other printed
material. This can create a package that's more valuable than
the individual parts would be on their own.

NUMBER 21: subliminal self-hypnosis products. We had
a joint venture with a gentleman a few years ago where we
created subliminal self-help tapes on things like quitting smoking
and losing weight. The audio was produced in such a way to help
reprogram the mind. You can do things like that with audio—
subliminal, self hypnosis, self-help programs that deliver
whatever the message is that you're trying to deliver.

NUMBER 22: Now we're into video-type products, specifically live recorded speeches, seminars, and consultations. We just talked about this with audio. Here at M.O.R.E., Inc. we regularly host one-day live events; and at least once a year, and sometimes more often, we have a three-day event where we and our guest speakers get up on stage and talk about making money. **Most of that is recorded on audio, but a lot is also recorded on video. A video can be digital, so it could be delivered via email, website or YouTube; or it can be delivered on a DVD that people can watch on their TV or computer.** Either way, it's still video, and it's very valuable as an information product.

NUMBER 23: Video how-to instructionals. This would be something like what Chris did for our websites, as outlined in the discussion for Number 17. **Think of all the things that you're good at or that you know about, and there are people who might be interested in buying information on that.** Chris tells me that he uses instructional videos all the time as a consumer himself, mostly stuff posted on YouTube; **a lot of the content is free these days, because people are using it to build a list or to try to sell something else.** In fact, just a couple of weeks ago, he got a new system set up to record audio into his computer directly. He has a professional-grade boom microphone sitting right in front of him, so he went on YouTube and watched a video about that piece of hardware, so that he could figure out how to configure it to get the best sound out of it. Basically, he was using a video information product to learn how to configure his microphone to record audio products.

NUMBER 24 takes us back to interviews, conversations, and roundtable discussions, but on video this time. If Eileen and I were doing the $2,500 Weekend project today, we might record video as well as audio, because of **the value of having multiple channels of distribution.** We could produce an interview-style conversation for video publication on DVD or on the Internet, as well as the audio that could be sold or given away—or all the things you could do with that content, as well. And again, don't just think about what you're capable of doing on your own. Because you may think, "I don't have anybody to interview." Or, "I'm not an expert at much of anything." That's no knock on you; that may be reality. But what you can do is get some other person to be your spokesperson, the individual talking on camera.

Let's say, for example, that you get someone to interview someone else, and you record it. You're the publisher. You're the producer. You're just providing the content to people who you know are interested in it. Or maybe you can do the interviews yourself; maybe you've always wanted to learn about XYZ. What you could do is follow your curiosity and interview somebody expert on the subject, making a deal to split the profits with them on any information product you create from that interview. **Remember, you can convert it into a wide variety of formats, including print, rather than just video or audio.** There's huge potential there.

And NUMBER 25, our final item for this chapter, **is video interactive with a workbook.** Again, this would be as part of a home study course of some kind, where you produce a video series that comes with a workbook. **The video walks the viewer through the print material. It's part of a bigger package, and you can even add an audio option to the package if you like.**

Product Evolution

The above categories represent just a few of the ways you can develop audio/video products. You're likely to come up with many other ideas to exploit. **One of the best things about deciding that you want to do audio or video publishing is that once you've developed a passion for using those media, you're going to find other ways to use them.** At the very least, you can rerecord them as technology advances. Think about it; the video of 20 years ago or even 10 years ago isn't the video of today, because of the current availability of high-speed Internet and online editing tools and other things that make it easy to produce video on the Internet. We don't know where video and audio is going to be 10 years from now or even five years from now. There may be new methods of getting your audio or your video into the marketplace.

So don't be boxed in by just a few ideas. **Just embrace the concept of adding video and audio to your information marketing business; the exact way you deliver that content may change over time.** You may come up with something creative that none of us have even thought of before. These are just starter ideas that I've presented here, to help you jump in with both feet. I honestly believe that all this is going to get easier and cheaper and faster. We never know where this trend is going to end up, and it's going to be exciting to find out.

Here's an interesting example of a unique kind of information product. We have a friend, Eric Bechtold, who goes paragliding. Basically, he flies around on this little glider with a motor attached. He can take off in a very limited space and fly all around for hours. **He's actually taken video of himself**

talking to his customers while he's in the air, 1,000 feet off the ground. Here's something else extreme: the wife of one of our staff members is turning 50 tomorrow. He bought her some tickets to go skydiving. **One of the things that this skydiving service will do as a premium is videotape his wife jumping out of an airplane.** See what I mean here? It's going to get easier and easier to do all of this stuff!

Even if you're in introverted person, like me, you can tap into it. I'm a loner and enjoy long hours by myself; I'm never lonely. Yet I can also be a very outgoing, extroverted kind person when I'm in front of a group. But I've dealt with a lot of nervousness over the years. **I used to get so nervous 10-15 years ago that I would throw up before some of our big events.** Now, I've watched myself on video from some of those early years, when I *knew* that I was scared to death, when I was absolutely frightened beyond belief when I was up on stage being interviewed—and this just goes back as little as seven or eight years ago, when we brought in professional video people to record some of our events. I just felt like I was under a lot of pressure at the time. But when I go back and look at myself on the video, there's no way I can even remotely tell how nervous I was. I **just come across as excited, passionate, animated, and enthusiastic.** No one could really tell I was nervous, not even the people around me at the time, like Chris Lakey.

And here's another thing about nervousness: once you really get into something, nervousness goes away. That's my experience, at least, and I'm assuming that some of you are like me: you're somewhat introverted, which is why you're a writer to begin with. Well, for years we've done these two- and three-day seminars, where the first few hours are like a living nightmare for me, because I'm kind of scared, at first, when I'm in front of large groups of people. But after a while my nervousness goes away. and I start getting into the process and I really enjoy it.

Last year, we had a seminar in Dallas, with a whole bunch of our customers there. Now, I'm usually okay speaking in front of 20 or 30 people; but if you put a whole roomful of people together, it kind of scares me. Well, I decided I wasn't going to do this anymore. **I made a decision that I was going to enjoy the event from the very first minute.** I was still nervous, so I walked on the treadmill for a while like I always do, trying to work out some of my nerves before I had to speak.

I started with this high-energy song that I had our sound man play over his system... and I came out and just made a total ass out of myself in front of the whole group. You see, a lot of the nervousness you feel when speaking before big groups—at least for me—is being scared of what other people are going to think about you. So I got that out of the way from the beginning. I had the sound man play this song, and then I just started dancing the room. I danced for about five minutes, and made a total ass out of myself—**and later, I told the group why. I told them about how nervous I am in front of large groups, and I told them that I was so afraid that I was going to screw up and make a jerk out of myself, so I decided I was just going to be a jerk right away and eliminate my fear.** The customers loved it!

So you see, you don't have to be a professional. **You just have to be real.**

Let me repeat that quote from earlier: **"The information**

business does not require talent, just an understanding of your market and a little work." Some of the highest-paid information marketers are boring to listen to. I can think of one very successful guy who's made millions of dollars in this field—and yet he's boring. He doesn't even try to act enthusiastic at all. I *hate* that. I can't stand a speaker who just mumbles on and on, who doesn't even try to act enthusiastic... and yet that's what this guy does. That's his whole style. **Now, whatever he lacks in enthusiasm he makes up for in the fact that he's real, he's raw, he's very truthful, and he's an authority on the subject.** His customers still love him, but trying to trying to listen to him hour after hour is pretty damn boring, I can you that!

And this fellow that I spent $397 on recently is from the Deep South. He's got one hell of an accent, and yet who cares how he sounds? I love the guy. He's real, he's raw, he tells it like it is, and it's a subject that I'm very interested in and want to know more about. **I like his style of teaching, and I could care less if he stutters a little or has a really thick accent.** Most people are the same way, because what they're paying for is results. **They want value, and they don't care how you sound or how professional you are as long as you give them that value.**

Our customers loved our first audio program, the $2,500 Weekend, because it gave them tremendous value. **The idea behind that program was so simple that it was brilliant; and truly, most of the ideas that make the most money are really simple.** They have to be simple for people to grasp them. We put our simple idea into play, charging just $195 for something we'd paid $2,500 for—and it was our first million-selling product. It was poorly recorded, kind of embarrassing to listen to now, and yet it represented real value to our customers.

No sooner did we get that one done that I recorded a 20-cassette series called *Millionaire Mastermind*. This was in 1990, and I did it without any help from anybody. I'd been listening to a lot of cassettes, and I wanted to do it myself so badly. I would wake up in the morning, spend about an hour taking notes, then spread all my notes around me. **Remember: it all starts with the writing. Then, for every hour that I would write notes, I would record about an hour of audio.** We still give that product away. We don't sell it anymore; we just give it away as a free bonus now.

For years we had a group of people, Chris Lakey among them, who got together every single week and recorded new programs—hundreds of them over the years. At one time there were 14 of us, and any particular roundtable discussion consisted of anywhere from four or five of us to as many as 14. That went on for about 10 years. Again, we still use those programs today; we don't sell them individually now, but **we often give them away as bonuses. We sell special licensing packages for them, too.** Some of the material's a little outdated and, quite frankly, we're much better communicators now than we used to be. But we still use them in our business.

Then there are our monthly seminars, mostly monthly workshops where we'll just bring in 20 or 30 of our clients. Most are local clients, within a day's drive. Those clients are like our studio audience. It's nice to have a group of people you can communicate to. In front of a live group, the energy's a little different than it is with a studio-recorded product; and in some ways, recording an audio program in front of a group of people makes it better. **It's a good experience for them, because they're the first to get the materials.** Everybody likes to be the first. And of course, it's good for us, too. **It lets us spend time with our customers face-to-face; and nothing can replace staying close to your core market. It's very important to stay grounded that way.** So we record for 20 or 30 people at these events; but then those recordings go out to hundreds or, in some cases, even thousands of customers and prospects.

We try to stick to our areas of expertise, but we've also recorded a lot of programs on subjects we don't really know anything about. Real estate, for example: **we recorded about 50 hours worth of audio where we interviewed all these real estate experts.** I don't especially like making money with real estate, but our customers were interested in it, and so we did it. There are so many people out there selling their real estate programs, so we interviewed a bunch of them, and at the end of each interview, we provided their contact information. **It was great for them; nobody turned us down.** Every real estate expert we asked to be part of this said yes.

Whatever subject you can think of, there are all kinds of people out there who have books or other products associated with it. They're trying to become famous. They're trying to sell their stuff. They have products and services that they're trying to push. **In most cases, they're happy to be interviewed, because it makes it easier for them to sell their products.**

Then we did a big eBay course. We didn't know anything about eBay at the time, but we interviewed all these experts who did. That was right around 2005, when eBay was just exploding, really becoming popular and hot. We were able to give our customers a hell of a great audio program on how to make money with eBay, even though we didn't know anything about eBay ourselves.

And by the way: I want to point out that the notes and other documents that you put together for your audios can also be used to craft the advertising copy that you use to sell the audios. Think about that. If you're going to write a book, you would usually write an outline, a skeleton of ideas if you will, first. **If you're going to produce a bunch of audio and want to keep it focused, you might also have an outline of sorts. You could use that as your starter copy for your sales material.**

Do Your Market Research

If you're ever confused about what to do or where to go when putting together your own information products, buy some of someone else's. Get on some of these people's mailing lists. **Find out what they're doing.** In a way, this is what I did when I spent $397 on that one fellow's whole back catalog recently. I do that all the time, and you should too, just to stay grounded in what's working for other people. **Emulate the winners, because all these things I'm telling you are just abstract ideas until you actually see other people doing them.** You can easily see what they're doing simply by getting on their mailing lists and continuing to buy from them. Information sellers are everywhere, especially now that the Internet has taken off as it has. But don't let that discourage you. Let that *excite* you. There's a hell of a market out there for info products.

If you already have an information marketing business and you've never done that, you definitely need to. **I would encourage you to start building your library of other people's products, because they can help you think about**

how you can best incorporate audio or video into your existing business. Sam Walton, the man who started Wal-Mart, said he spent more time in K-Mart than the K-Mart executives. His point was that he knew his competition inside and out. He spent a lot of time determining what his main competitor (at the time) was doing. Now, I'm not necessarily talking about spying on your competition here... although that's a side benefit of doing business with your competitors. **The main goal is to see what's out there being sold in your marketplace. How are other companies incorporating these concepts into their businesses?**

I think you'll find that a lot of them are doing a poor job at it, actually, and you can beat them just by doing it better and being more committed to it. In the process, you'll also be able to get some ideas for the types of content to deliver, and the methods that are being used to deliver that content. **And you can learn some valuable lessons for free on the Internet.** Information marketing has undergone some transformation in the past few years, since the Internet really just exploded. It used to be that, in order to get information, you either read a book at the library, or you might buy a book. **These days, it's easy to get information for free on the Internet.**

If you want to study how to make marketing and information-based video and audio programs, just do some searching on the Internet. Go to your favorite search engine and search for "audio information products," or search for specific products. **You'll see a lot of people on the Internet using audio and video to get their presentations across to their clients, and even delivering full information programs via audio and/or video. You can learn a lot by watching them.**

I think what you'll also learn is the principle that we talked about earlier—that you don't have to be an expert speaker, you don't have to look like a Hollywood star, that you don't have to sound the best. **You just need to deliver good content.** If you'll do that, it doesn't matter what you look like. It doesn't matter how you sound. I'm not saying people might not make fun of you or laugh a little bit when they're listening, but they'll buy. They don't care. **They're looking for the content, not how you look or how you sound.** So don't let that stop you. If *it* is going to stop you, just pay your cousin or somebody else to do it for you. Maybe you'll like the way they look or sound better. **The point is, don't be afraid to incorporate audio and video into your business because it can be very profitable for you.**

And remember: these are just starter ideas, a few ways that can help you get going if you want to use audio or video. There are so many other things that you can do. **These are versatile formats, offering a lot of potential and options for reaching your marketplace and making more money. And it's not too hard to do a decent job of it.** The more you see other people doing it and doing a bad job, and not letting that stop them because it's still profitable—it's just a confidence booster! You look around and say, "Man, I can do better than that." **So spy on your competition. It's easier than ever to find out what other people are doing. Get on their mailing lists and start buying stuff from them.**

And last but not least, let me just wrap this up by, again, reminding you that many people choose to become writers because of the artistic, creative nature of writing. You want to tap into that. That's a big part of why you write in the first place. **I believe that information marketing is the ultimate way to**

make money with your creative powers. You get an idea, and you can turn it into a product and turn that into cashflow very quickly. Audio and even video are so easy that you can come up with an idea today and have money coming in within 30 days. And it's an idea that *you* came up with; you created it yourself. Remember the $2,500 Weekend, that first information product idea that made us a million bucks. It was a simple idea. I got in the shower one morning, had this simple little idea, and all of a sudden, we made over a million bucks.

Let that inspire you a little bit. **Realize that you're only limited by your imagination. The reason you chose to become a writer in the first place is because you want to tap into that creative part of you.** There's no better way to do it than to be in the information marketing business. So keep that in mind, and turn to the next chapter, where we'll wrap up this section on information marketing (and the book) by giving you some more specific examples of information products, and by putting a cap on all of this.

Electronic and Other Options

This is our final chapter on the types of information products that you can create for your business, as the profitable third way of getting paid to write. We're still working from our list of 40... even though we've already talked about several that aren't even on this list. And remember, these are just the basic formats; there are all kinds of variations here. Information can pretty much be presented any way you want it to be, which is one of the coolest things about selling information. So before we finish our list, let's just talk a little bit more about why you should be interested in selling information, and why it's such a cool way to make money with writing.

Controlling the Perception

I've already mentioned that perception is reality; and you really need to understand that, with information marketing, you control the perception. For example, what does a product that looks like a book sell for? Well, I've got one little book that I bought from a fellow named Peter McWilliams for $95. Peter passed away a while back, but when he was alive, I was one of his best customers. This is a little five-and-a-half by eight-and-a-half inch paperback book, maybe 170 pages long, but it's immensely valuable because it covers what he learned in a long, fruitful career of self-publishing. And even though it's just a little book that would normally sell for $12 or maybe as much as $14.95, he sold it for $95; in fact, he sold it as the most expensive book of its kind in the world.

Again, perception is reality; that's how Peter sold his book. And of course, he had the goods to back it up, because he was one of the most successful self-publishers in history. He sold millions and millions of copies of various kinds of books, and **that little book that I paid $95 for gave me the best of the best of everything he'd learned in the process. It was worth it to me.** I devoured that book—whereas if I *hadn't* paid $95 for it, I might have just skimmed it. I definitely got my money's worth.

And that's another cool thing about information, by the way. Information buyers are just insatiable. They're looking for results. They want answers—and for the most part, they don't care what it costs. **They'll pay for results, and they can't get enough.** In a nice way, they get addicted to buying information; they spend a lot of money on it. They collect this stuff, and they all have their favorite information sellers. **The more they buy, the more they *want* to buy.** Every purchase inflames their desire to purchase more. God only knows how many millions of buyers there are out there for information products, but thankfully, once they start buying the stuff, they don't stop. **And they'll continue to buy from you, because your information products are an extension of who you are.** To me, that's the ultimate competitive advantage: because we're living in a day and age when the market is cluttered and crowded, with so many people selling similar products and services. There's not enough differentiation between one and another.

If you're trying to build bonds with your customers, trying to get them to come back again and again, and all you do is sell the same type of stuff that everybody else sells—well, that's really hard to do. **But with information, you really are selling products that are an extension of you, especially if they're audio and video—because you have to be a very, very talented writer in order to truly connect with people through the written word.** You can do it, though, if you can inject enough of your personality into the copy to draw people in, so that you give them a real feeling of who you are and what you're all about. That's enhanced if you're using video and audio, because people start to feel like they know you even more.

So in an overcrowded world of "Me Too" companies that are all pretty much doing the same thing, selling information is the king, the key to profitability. **It's the greatest product possible.** And as I've been telling you all along, it's the ultimate creative way to make money. I am extremely aware that the average buyer of this book (and the audio program it's based on) is somebody who wants to get paid to write. You're probably thinking about traditional ways of writing, specifically of fiction. Even if you're not, I do know that part of what connects all writers is that we're looking for a creative outlet. **We're looking for a way to express ourselves in a creative, artistic way.**

There are many different ways that you can exercise that creativity. No matter which writing style you choose—whether you're into information marketing, whether you go the ghostwriting or copywriting route, whatever you're interested in—**this business gives you an excellent creative outlet.**

When I think of the opposite of creativity, I think of the factory worker and the person who pushes the same button, over and over again, all day long, to make a machine do what it's supposed to do. It's repetitive. They put in their four hours. The time clock buzzes and it's time for a 15-minute break. After the break is over, they go back to pushing the same buttons over and over again until lunch time. After lunch they go back and they do the same thing again, all day long. Then they punch out and go home. Then they come back the next day and do the same thing over and over again.

That's the opposite of what I'm talking about here. With the writing business, no matter what kind of writing you're doing, you're releasing your creativity. And there are all kinds of ways to exercise that creativity, so the projects you work on change on a daily basis, or maybe a weekly or monthly basis. Even if you're working on a lengthy project that takes several weeks or a month or more, there's always something new out to work on. **I think that most information marketers and other people using these strategies have multiple projects they're working on at any given time.** So for example, I may have one project that's taking me several weeks to do; but all the time I'm working on that big project, I've got little projects that come and go, or at least other things I'm working on. **So you *do* get to exercise that creativity.**

I just feel that this is the ultimate creative way to make money, because you're coming up with ideas constantly for products and services, and then you're creating them. Once you get good at it, you can create them rather quickly, and they can sell for a lot of money. **The profit margin is just incredible; it's outrageous.** For instance, we've sold seminars for thousands of dollars. What does it cost to put on a seminar? Well, your main cost is the marketing to promote the seminar really. After that, you have a fixed cost, whether you sell 10 seats or 100. You've got the hotel conference room and associated expenses. But if you manage your marketing right, you can walk away with the kind of money that most doctors and lawyers dream of making.

Selling Yourself Profitably

So all this can in fact be extremely creative, lucrative, fun, challenging, rewarding, and fulfilling. I hope I've got that idea across to you by now! Again, I'm very sensitive to the fact that you probably didn't really buy this product to learn how to be involved in all aspects of information marketing. You're interested in writing. And yet, the more you write about a subject, the easier it's going to be for you to communicate effectively through other media, such as audio or video. These media still involve writing at the highest level... and that brings me to the next thing.

All three of the money-making methods I've talked about in this book—copywriting, ghostwriting and information marketing—can be linked so that you're cashing in on all of them, not just one of them. That's our story. As I've already mentioned, the audios that we created for the original *Get Paid to Write* audio program went straight to our ghostwriter, who turned them into the printed product you're holding in your hand. In addition to a book, they'll probably be used in newsletters, and any other way that we can think of. I hope you can see how that connects.

Perhaps you never thought about being an information marketer as such. But understand that if you're a writer, you're probably selling yourself as a writer... which makes you a kind of information marketer anyway. Let's say you're a ghostwriter, writing for other people. Well, how do you go about doing that?

How do you sell your services? **One way is to create information products that allow people to get to know you, so they can sample some of the things you can do for them.** Do you see how these things can be interrelated? If you're a copywriter, you could be writing for other people exclusively; but a lot of copywriters write for themselves as well. In any case, they're selling their own services by way of writing sales copy to sell themselves and their abilities to others. If you're an information marketer, you're probably writing your own sales copy to sell your information products. Of course, it's possible that you're not using all these methods together; **but I think, inasmuch as you want to make as much money as possible, you're probably mixing some of them anyhow. That's what allows you to make the most money.**

There's really no limit to the amount of ways that you can make money in the writing industry; it's up to you to just decide what you want to do and go for it. Hopefully, some of the strategies and ideas that we've shared with you in this product cause you to rethink what you thought you knew about making money as a writer, and even challenge you to be more creative in how you think about marketing yourself.

I know of a copywriter named Bob Bly. He's published a bunch of different books and other information products on copywriting. Now, Bob is a freelance copywriter. In between jobs, I imagine, is when he writes his own books and other information products. So here's a wildly successful freelance copywriter who also publishes independent material on copywriting with the understanding that this makes him an expert... which helps him get *more* freelance work. **This is a marketing strategy; he's selling himself even as he profits**

from his freelance work. I've seen other experts do this, too.

There are just so many ways to combine your creativity to generate profits; and you know, **the amount of money that you can generate by using these methods to create successful information products can be staggering.** That little booklet that we first wrote back in 1988, *Dialing for Dollars,* sold 160,000 copies in the original version; and of course, we kept improving and adding to it. Finally, there were two volumes, whereas it started out as a thin little brochure. By the time the promotion died out four or five years later, we had a big, thick package that we sold.

That first million-dollar product idea that we had, the $2,500 Weekend, generated $1.5 million in sales. It only took us one weekend to create—and that was a weekend where we were doing a bunch of other things, too. It consisted of about six hours of finished audio, with no real editing—just stopping and starting the tape player for a weekend. Of course, it did take me several months to write the sales letter... but that same sales letter, today, would take me a week or 10 days to do, at the most. **When you look at the number of hours that you put into a product like this one, versus the amount of money that you can get out of it, the profit is incredible—almost unbelievable.** And yet it's real... and you can prove that to yourself with the right product.

There's a lot of potential in the industry as a whole to simply pick the amount of money you want to make based on the lifestyle you want to live, what you want to do with your money, and how active you want to be. You can work part-time, or even from a retired or semi-retired perspective. Maybe you just want to share what you know from a lifetime of business, so maybe you do some light coaching. Maybe you write books. Maybe you get yourself interviewed, and create some information products that way.

If you're retired, maybe you're just looking to supplement your income a little after a lifetime of work, while you enjoy not being very busy. Other people make this a full time business; they work it 100 hours a week, and it's their life. They're loving what they do, so they do it all the time. Maybe they work out of their home; or maybe they're a circuit speaker, earning their living developing information products and speaking before big groups of people on an almost nightly basis. **How you want to handle things, and sell yourself profitably, is all up to you, so give some serious thought to the options available based on what you'd like to achieve.**

Opportunities, Educational and Otherwise

One more thing before we go on to the list: **be aware that there's a huge amount of good information out there on information marketing.** Back in 1988, when we got started in the business, there was very little. Russ von Hoelscher had a book called *How to Sell Information by Mail*, and there were a few other little books available, but that was really it. Now, thanks to the Internet, the information marketing world has exploded with growth—and there are so many people out there willing to help. There's also the Information Marketing Association, which you'll definitely want to check out.

Otherwise, there are also many people you can emulate, even some who don't call themselves information marketers. For example, I've mentioned that we didn't think of ourselves as information marketers in the very beginning. We thought of ourselves as being in the self publishing business. Nowadays, we mostly equate that concept with people who publish only their own books and other documents, and the truth is, information marketing encompasses so much more. **So there _are_ many role models for you to choose from; but remember, don't let their huge numbers turn you off! That's a definite plus, not a minus.** It means there's a profitable market there. Information buyers tend to be insatiable, so not only are they buying from all these other people, they'll buy from you also.

I'd like you to keep these main themes in mind as you continue reading this chapter, which is why I've re-emphasized them here, even though I've talked about them a bit before. As you consider getting into the writing business, **one of the key things that you must remember is that once you've identified a buyer for your information and sold something to them, that person is likely to continue buying information on the same or similar subjects from you.** Surely, by now, you've thought a lot about the ways that you would like to see yourself making a living writing. So whatever thing you have in mind, whatever you've been mulling over or kicking around in your head, just know that whatever marketplace that is, when it comes to information that they're interested in, **they'll buy it in all kinds of forms and sizes and variances as long as it's related to that main theme they're interested in.**

For example, one of the things that we do is teach direct mail marketing to businesses. We know that a small business owner who buys one of our direct marketing products and likes what they've read is likely to be interested in an audio program we have on the same subject. Or they might be interested in something that's a bit different, but also still in the same direct mail genre. So again, someone who buys once will most likely buy again... though they may not buy from *you* again. **Many factors go into that decision on whether they choose to continue doing business with you. But they *will* buy.** That's a factor for you to consider as you seek to do business with people.

Remember that people are mostly insatiable with their appetite for information. If you can harness that and get them to continue looking to you for that information, they'll continue to give you their money, as they continue to feed their appetite for knowledge and for more information on whatever it is that you're sharing with or revealing to them.

Let's move on to our last 15 products in our list of 40. Remember, this all comes from *The Official Get Rich Guide to Information Marketing*.

The Products

The first few items are Internet products... and of course, Internet products can be just like these other products we've already discussed. **NUMBER 26 happens to be an e-book, which is just a book that's in digital format.** These days, e-books are just as popular as regular, printed books. In fact, Amazon sells more digital versions of their books than they do traditional print books these days. It used to be that when you talked about e-books, you had to explain what that was; **but these days people *prefer* e-books.** Most are delivered via specialized devices, like Amazon's own Kindle book reader. Even mobile phones have book reader apps these days. If you're an Apple user, you'll find an e-reader app at the Apple Store; there's even an Apple e-book store, iBooks, where you can find your own copies of e-books. **I believe any publisher is welcome**

to publish to those formats. There are numerous options for delivering your book digitally over the Internet via those outlets, but beyond that **you can also deliver your own e-book via a website.** You just have to format it as a downloadable product — for example, a PDF file or something similar.

NUMBER 27 is downloadable products such as manuals and audio. There's no limit to what this could be, really; in fact, **these days a lot of people are delivering by download what they used to deliver exclusively via print.** Some of our own manuals and audio products are delivered via the Internet now. Whatever you were delivering offline by mail, you can now deliver online. It's so easy to tell people, "Just visit our website, and you can download any of this content that you want." Some of it we give away for free; some of it requires a purchase or an opt-in, where they're providing their contact information in exchange for receiving this digital content. Because it's downloadable, the delivery costs are essentially nothing; that makes this format very attractive. I will warn you, though: sometimes that means the perceived value is also lower, so you need to build up the value. You have to make it so that it still has a high perceived value.

NUMBER 28 is a membership site. This is something where customers are allowed to access information via a password-protected website or a secure location on the Internet. We deliver some content that's protected behind a password. A membership site could be a monthly thing, where they pay a monthly fee to access the content; or it could be a one-time fee. Whatever it is, they're accessing the information based on the fact that they earned the right, through some payment, to receive the information that's hidden behind this password protected area.

NUMBER 29 (and this is the final topic for Internet products) **is structured lessons of some kind.** This is where customers are led through a series of lessons; these may also include tests, examinations, quizzes, and things like that. **Again, there are websites that deliver education via this method.** One of Chris Lakey's daughters does some online lessons through the Internet. She has a password and a login. She goes through lessons, and can be quizzed on things. Similarly, some friends of Chris home school their children, and it's all done via an Internet website for home schoolers. The kids go through the material at their own pace, and when they're done, they take the quizzes online and teachers review their work.

You can do that with information as well. It doesn't necessarily have to be what you'd think of as schooling, per se. **It could just be educational information products delivered via a website that's structured in nature, so there's Lesson 1, Lesson 2, Lesson 3.** If we were to make this particular program into such a product, we would have lessons on getting paid to write as a ghostwriter, and then we'd have lessons on copywriting, on information publishing, and things like that. They'd be broken down into bite-sized pieces and delivered over a set period of weeks, or months, or however long you chose to handle that. **People could pay for access (sort of combining this with the membership idea), but have these structured lessons delivered systematically via the Internet.** Again, when you compare it to the cost of traditionally delivering these things by mail or administering them offline, you can save a lot of money, which can translate into greater profits if you handle it right.

That's the end of our Internet section; the final category is more or less miscellaneous, general ideas that don't neatly fit into any of the other categories mentioned here. **The first, NUMBER 30, is trainer kits: that is, multimedia kits for use in conducting classes, workshops, etc.—just information products full of training materials.** The next one, **NUMBER 31, is memberships.** It could be a membership in anything. Over the years, we've been involved with many memberships that people pay a fee for—like the Information Marketing Association, which we've been members of since the beginning. **A membership could be as simple as you delivering a newsletter to members, a regular publication with members-only content.**

NUMBER 32 is devices. This is an interesting one. The listed example is something called a stress card. And here's something I'll just throw out as a concept. Chris Lakey's wife and daughter are getting ready to travel to China to work with some orphans in summer camps, so they've been raising money for their travels. **One of the things they sold was a little pizza card that the local Papa John's gave them: buy one pizza, get one free.** It's good all year long. They're absolutely free for the nonprofit, as long as they're raising money for some nonprofit purpose. These cards sold for $10. You could see what a good deal that was for the buyer, right? Well, it was a good deal for the sellers, too. The team got $10 every time they sold one, and the cards were given to them free.

So in a sense, that was a device. **That's what we're talking about here: something used for a specific purpose that wouldn't necessarily be a traditional information product, though of course it's a printed card.** It could be a pet-finder thing. One of our marketing buddies out in California had a pet-finder information product that came with something like that. There was a little card, and tags that the pet could wear around their neck. A client's pet's information was logged into the system. Anytime their pet turned up missing, they could find out, hopefully, where it was; assuming that someone would report that to the pet-finder system so they would be able to locate their animal. It's information still, but it's provided by means of some kind of device.

And here's something that we've done with a copywriting program that we sold a few years ago. **As part of that course, we included these laminated sheets that provided our best copywriting tips, tricks, and strategies.** The course sold for hundreds of dollars, and then with it came these laminated sheets and manuals and such, so that when you opened the box it was like Christmas when you were a kid. People love that kind of thing; they can't get enough of it.

NUMBER 33 is plaques—I suppose this would be informational signs or rewards of the kind that you might hang on your wall. This is something that we've never done.

NUMBER 34 is computer software. That's pretty self-explanatory. If you're a programming geek, you could write your own software; or you could hire someone to do it for you. There's a website called Elance.com where you can post a request for a bid, asking how much someone would charge for programming a piece of software for you. You tell them what you want it to do, and they'll give you a quote for what it costs. You accept the bid, wait a while, and out comes this software. **Once you pay for it, it's yours. You can package it up and sell it via a website, or via mail, or however you wanted to do**

that. So even if you're not a programmer, you can make money with information that would be delivered via computer software.

NUMBER 35 is specially-priced packages of a variety of related information products: things like books, reports, audio, or DVDs, all packaged together and sold for a special price. If you're a musician, you could package three of your top discs together, and sell them that way. Whereas normally they would sell for $10 each, you might sell them for $25 — $5 off for the set.

NUMBER 36: continuity programs involving multiple information products, or multiple media. Again, you're basically packaging a bunch of different things together. It could be that you have a membership service, like I've already talked about, and that membership includes some audio, some print, some video, some online access. Maybe it includes some newsletters, e-books, or some other downloadable content. **All of these different kinds of information can be packaged together and delivered on a regular basis.** Or it could be something like a coaching program, where automatic continuity is built in every month. Whatever it is, you're charging people regularly to continue getting the content.

NUMBER 37 is services, which could be tied to memberships or purchased as premiums. I suppose coaching programs might fall into that category. **Rather than a product, a tangible thing, you're selling a service, or at least a benefit that's more service-oriented than physically delivered.** We've done lots of coaching programs. In fact, we're doing some new coaching programs that are like miniature versions of our normal ones: they're six-week, eight-week, 10-week programs that people can easily get into without making any long term commitment, so the sales are hot.

NUMBER 38: customized information to different marketplaces or different clients. We've made money over the years selling customized websites, where the person's able to build a website to their specifications. We also sell replicated websites to some of our clients, where they're all the same and there's no customization; they're pretty much all cookie cutter, so to speak. **So you could sell customized information, where you're working with different groups of people and personalizing things or customizing them based on needs, or whatever people are looking for.**

NUMBER 39 is private label items. You can private label your own information for other marketers. You can also buy private label rights from other people and have new products to sell that you didn't create on your own. I could spend multiple chapters talking about private label options; but **the short story is that if you have your own information products, whether they fall into one of these categories or others, you could private label them for other people to use.** For example, if you have reports, you can allow people to private label your reports, so that there's nothing specific to your company in there. You allow them to put their own name on it and sell it or give it away, whatever you choose to license them the rights to do. Audio programs, software, any of these things can be licensed or private labeled to other people to use.

You get a royalty or an up-front payment of some kind—whatever you agree to—and they get the rights to the product. It gives them the ability to get started without having to do all the work themselves. You've already done the work, and you're just licensing it to them. And as I said, the flip of that can also work to your advantage. **If you're looking to expand your product line, you can acquire the rights to private label someone else's information.** If you've got a built-in marketplace of people who've already been responsive, you can take someone else's product, slap your own brand on it, pay them a royalty fee for the rights to do it, and instantly go out there and have a product to sell to your marketplace.

In fact, we did this one time. We spent about $100,000 for the rights to one CD, and I think we got six other ones for $125,000 total. The content on those discs was extremely valuable. We knew our clients would pay us a premium price for the information that was on those CDs; **we had a built-in marketplace for it, so it was worth it to us to pay that kind of money.**

All of our friends thought we were crazy to spend so much for the product. They thought we had more money than brains, and they made fun of us—and not even behind our backs! And yet, we also received a killer sales letter with that product, one that our joint venture partner had fully tested. He had made a bunch of money with this sales letter—and **we quickly made over a million dollars with that product, about ten times what we'd paid for it.** Then we sold other types of related products that *we* created, reusing that excellent sales letter that we bought as sort of the foundation for them. So, who had the last laugh? We did.

Now, that's an extreme example; typically, you might spend a few thousand dollars to buy the rights to products that can be privately labeled. In many cases, if you've already got clients who have proven they're interested in that kind of subject matter, they'll be willing to come back to you and buy new information. **So taking someone else's material and private labeling it can also be a source of revenue.**

NUMBER 40: Licensing for republication. This is similar to private labeling, except that the products are licensed for a specific use. For example, you don't really own the operating system that's on your computer. You license it from Microsoft, assuming you're using a Windows-based computer. They allow you to use it, and that license controls what you can and can't do with it.

As with private labeling, this can go both ways. You can sell a license to someone else to sell your information or, if you're looking for additional revenue, you can license someone else's products and add them to your own product line. Let's say I wanted to sell something that was branded with the Apple logo. I would not be private labeling it; I would be licensing it. I'm not trying to say it's my computer brand; it's an Apple brand, but you're buying it from me.

We've sold a ton of distributorships and joint ownership packages where, essentially, we're just licensing rights to all of our products to someone else; that is, we give people a certificate of ownership, so to speak, along with samples of the products. **The profit margins are just incredibly high.**

Tips on Getting Started

There you have it: Numbers 26 through 40. **There are many, many variations within those categories.** If you're really interested in producing information products, there's no end to the types, the quantities, the sizes, the shapes, and all the other factors you can take advantage of. **Again, the main thing here is to find the things that interest you the most and run with them.** Just pick the first information product and get started; the others will come. Start with one and branch out from there. **Just use your imagination, and let your marketplace tell you what they're interested in the most.** Any of these things can be profitable.

Who knows? Maybe something I've written in this chapter inspired a million dollar idea for you. You just have to find it and then run with it. **Once you do find something that interests you, offer it to a rabid market. And be sure it *is* something you like, because that makes it so much more fun and creative.** I'd hate to get involved in something I didn't enjoy— and that's exactly what someone approached me with recently. He wanted me to get started in a whole different business. This is a man who, at one point, was just about a billionaire. He lost most of his fortune—that's a whole other story—and now, he's actually helping people get involved in that business that made him almost a billionaire. But I have no interest in that business, none whatsoever. It's something that I would hate. I think I can do much better in markets I'm passionate about, and I think the same is true for you, too.

Combine that passion with a rabid marketplace, where people are starving for information, and you'll be in money-making heaven every day. That's the way the market is moving now; the profit margins are incredible. People love the impulsive nature of it—the fact they can pay their money now and instantly get something that's of real value to them. **The more ways that you can provide that information they value, the better.** It gives you a freedom and flexibility that you don't have

with a traditional business. As an example, by the 1990s we had
developed 148 different information products that we sold in our
catalog. This was back when we had cassette tapes, manuals,
and many of the other kinds of items I've talked about in the last
few chapters. Well, a lot of that information is a little bit
outdated now—but the core secrets and methods and strategies
we covered are all still useful. **So now, instead of delivering it
as a mountain of manuals and cassettes, we put it all on a
DVD. We also put it online, which makes it even easier.**

We've got a manual right now that's almost 1,000 pages; it
literally took me 10 years to write it. Seriously, I just wrote a
little bit every day for 10 years. Just to attract the right kind of
buyers that we're looking for, we're giving it away for free now.
**We want to just blow people's minds. We want them to get
this thing and be totally shocked and overwhelmed, because
we're trying to start relationships with them, and we feel
that there's no better way to do that than with the shock-
and-awe treatment.** And yet, because that manual is in PDF
form, and they can get it digitally, it doesn't cost us any real
money to give it to them. The only cost is in the marketing to get
people to go to the website, give us their full contact
information, and get that manual. **It doesn't cost us *anything*
extra.** That's very liberating compared to the old style; just
printing a 1,000-page manual costs about $20, especially if
you're printing them one at a time. When you deliver it digitally,
you don't have those high costs.

**There are just so many ways to package this stuff, and
you'll never run out of ideas, because it really is only limited
by your imagination.** It'll be wide open as long as you're
creative and you're looking at the marketplace with your eyes

open—and you're stealing the best ideas from other people. I don't mean that you should plagiarize, since that's unethical, but you should always be looking for ways to create and combine and be innovative.

The Bottom Line

Basically, that wraps up information marketing. **It's a phenomenal way to make money, extremely creative, and can be combined very effectively with the other two methods of writing that I've discussed in this book.** All of it works hand in hand.

In this book, I've done my best to share with you the greatest tips, tricks, and strategies that we've discovered and developed since 1988. **We're always learning.** This is the kind of thing where school is never out for the pro. Just when you think you know it all, somebody comes along, and they're doing something totally innovative that, all of a sudden, gets you excited again. There's always something to learn.

I hope you'll think about copywriting—and the fact that millions of businesses aren't getting enough sales and profits right now. They're frustrated, they're struggling, and they need somebody with writing talent who can also sell, whether it be on paper or websites or whatever—somebody who has some talent for creating copy that causes people to want to buy. This is a talent that a lot of business owners just don't have. They do have some experience in products and services that can help you when write compelling copy, or maybe they're great in some ways at selling stuff, but they've never taken recordings of their sales presentations and tried to put them in print or anything. **The opportunities for making**

money as a freelance copywriter are tremendous. As a copywriter selling your own products and services, again, you're only limited by your imagination.

As far as ghostwriters go, there's a consistent need there as well, for all of kinds of people who are famous, or want to become famous, or want to contribute something to their family, or their clients. If they're politicians, they want to get elected; if they're business owners, they want more sales and profits. **The opportunities for making money with ghostwriting are exceptional, so don't let the fact that there's already a bunch of people doing it discourage you.** Let that inflame your desire to want to do it.

The fact that there are so many people using all three of these writing methods to make money is actually a great thing. Don't ever sell yourself short in thinking that's not an asset; it's a *tremendous* asset. Only somebody who doesn't understand marketing and the insatiable demand in the marketplace looks at competition as a bad thing. Those of us who understand all this know that more is better. I hope you'll continue to think deeply about this until you do gain a firm understanding of it.

People are insatiable, and the fact that there are so many competitors indicates that the market is hot. It's hot for ghostwriting, it's hot for freelance copywriting, it's hot for all kinds of information marketing. I know you probably didn't buy this product thinking you were going to learn about these things per se, but I hope by now you realize this is a very creative way to make money. **In fact, I believe there's no more creative way to make money, as a writer, than by combining all three of these methods.** I assure you: once the money starts rolling in, you'll get more excited about the whole thing; and after you do it for a while you'll fall in love with it, and you'll never want to do anything else.

Hopefully, the things I've discussed here have generated some helpful thoughts about your own desires to get paid to write. I assume that you originally bought this product because you had some kind of a dream of making money as a writer, but maybe weren't sure how to get started—or even what kind of writing you wanted to do. Maybe when you got started, you just wanted to be a ghostwriter, or a copywriter; maybe information marketing wasn't something that was on your radar screen. I hope it is now.

If you do want to be a writer, if you honestly want to learn to make use of these methods, **I would encourage you to get started. If you want to write for other people, just start doing it. You'll improve inevitably as you go along.** When I stumble across old sales letters I wrote years ago, sometimes I look at them and realize that they're almost laughable, and I'm embarrassed a little. I wouldn't make the same mistakes today. **You learn as you go... and the truth is, a lot of those embarrassing sales letters made money.** So you don't have to be perfect to get started. Don't feel like you have to be a master of writing before you start making money at it. You just need to get out there and get started... and I would encourage you not to wait too long.

Chris Lakey has a bass guitar he's trying to learn to play. He's had it for a few years now. Now, his family is very musical, and his 14-year-old daughter can play guitar better than anybody else in his family. She prods Chris to try to learn bass, so they can play together a little more. He's done some learning. One of the things they suggest in the music world is that you play with people, as often as possible, even though you may stink; because the more you play, the get better you get. And the more you play with people, the more you learn how to play with and interact with them. Your music will come along a lot faster. Now, Chris isn't there yet. He just plugs out notes, he says; but it's kind of fun to play, especially when he's playing guitar with his daughter.

Writing is similar. The best way to get better is to just do it. Don't spend too much time trying to learn theory and style and technique. Now, I'm very appreciative that you purchased this *Get Paid to Write* product; don't get me wrong. I think that the product can be very helpful and instructive. That said, don't spend too long on your education before you just get out there and start doing it. **To some extent, the learning will come as you go.** Whatever you've decided you want to do, however you've decided you want to get paid to write, just start doing it. **Try to get those first jobs. Try to do something.** If you're writing for your own business, that's a lot easier, because you can just make the decision to start writing your own sales letters or creating your products for yourself.

Again, I would encourage you to just do it. **Just don't wait too long, or there will be all kinds of excuses in your way.** The doubt will creep in. People will tell you that you shouldn't do it yet, you're not ready, or that all these bad things can happen — and that can discourage you. Just get out there and do it.

And just to cap this off, **if you haven't thought about information marketing before, I want to encourage you to just spend a little more time thinking about it.** Because you can be a writer and an information marketer both. This won't keep you from doing those other things that, maybe, you thought of doing when you first purchased this product. **Information marketing gives you so much more versatility in what you do.** All you have to do to begin making money with information is to identify a group of people who really want that information, then develop the right way to give it to them. We've talked about all the different kinds of ways you can deliver content to people. **They'll spend a lot of money on information that they want, information that provides them with solutions or fixes for the problems they face.**

The marketplace is insatiable. **Every marketplace is insatiable for the right kind of information.** You can offer them solutions and make a lot of money doing it. **If your main purpose is just to figure out something that you can do to make money, do consider information marketing, because it's very lucrative.** And it's something that gives you a lot of options when it comes to selling information to a marketplace.

So I urge you to go back and read this book again, because you'll notice things you didn't before, or new ideas will be triggered that you missed the first time around. Mark up passages; highlight; write in the margins. Our best ideas will become your best ideas. **Once you've absorbed this information, go out and implement it. Don't wait for the perfect moment.** "Confidence is a plant of slow growth;" that's a quote from the 15th century. The point is, it takes time to develop your confidence; and you can earn as you learn. Get started. You can do it. There are so many other people out there doing it, having paved the way for you. Let them serve as good role models for you.

I hope you've enjoyed this book. I hope you feel like

you've gotten far more than your money's worth, because that was my goal. **Let us know how you're using these strategies. And of course, let us know if there's any way we can be of more assistance.** We're happy to help. We're here to help you every step of the way.

www.ingramcontent.com/pod-product-compliance
Lightning Source LLC
Chambersburg PA
CBHW020159200326
41521CB00005BA/194